THE ULTIMATE
BREVILLE SMART AIR FRYER OVEN
COOKBOOK

200+ QUICK AND EASY MOUTH-WATERING AIR FRYER OVEN RECIPES FOR HEALTHY EATING, FROM BREAKFAST TO DINNER. INCLUDING VEGETARIAN AND PALEO IDEAS

BESS NOWAK

INTRODUCTION 9

UNDERSTANDING BREVILLE SMART AIR FRYER OVEN 10

1. Breville Smart Air Fryer Oven 10
2. How to Prepare the Smart Oven Before the First Use .. 10
3. Smart Oven Air Fryer Features 11
4. Advantages of the Smart Air Fryer Oven 11
5. Care and Cleaning................... 12

BREAKFAST RECIPES 13

1. Basil Tomato Frittata 14
2. Italian Breakfast Frittata 14
3. Healthy Baked Omelette 15
4. Easy Egg Casserole 15
5. Flavor Packed Breakfast Casserole 16
6. Vegetable Sausage Egg Bake................ 16
7. Cheese Broccoli Bake 17
8. Cheese Ham Omelette................ 17
9. Sweet Potato Frittata 18
10. Squash Oat Muffins 18
11. Hashbrown Casserole 19
12. Mexican Breakfast Frittata 19
13. Perfect Brunch Baked Eggs 20
14. Green Chile Cheese Egg Casserole 20
15. Breakfast Salmon Patties 21
16. Zucchini Fries................ 21
17. Breakfast Stuffed Peppers................ 22
18. Crispy Breakfast Potatoes................ 22
19. Quick Cheese Omelet 23
20. Tomato Spinach Frittata................ 23
21. Ham Egg Brunch Bake 24
22. Roasted Brussels Sprouts & Sweet Potatoes 24
23. Roasted Potato Wedges 25
24. Breakfast Egg Bites................ 25
25. Grilled Cheese Sandwich 26

MAIN RECIPES 27

26. Grilled Cheese Sandwich 28

27. Italian Meatballs 28
28. Loaded Baked Potatoes 29
29. Pepperoni Pizza 30
30. Southern Style Fried Chicken 31
31. Stuffed Bell Peppers 32
32. Tuna Patties................ 33
33. Ham and Cheese Sandwich 33
34. Easy Hot Dogs 34
35. Japanese Chicken Mix 34
36. Prosciutto Sandwich 35
37. Lentils Fritters 35
38. Lunch Potato Salad 36
39. Corn Casserole 36
40. Bacon and Garlic Pizzas 37
41. Sweet and Sour Sausage Mix 37
42. Meatballs and Tomato Sauce 38
43. Stuffed Meatballs 38
44. Steaks and Cabbage 39
45. Succulent Lunch Turkey Breast 39
46. Italian Eggplant Sandwich 40
47. Creamy Chicken Stew................ 40
48. Lunch Pork and Potatoes 41
49. Bacon Cheddar Chicken Fingers................ 41
50. Battered Cod 42
51. Beef Kabobs................ 42
52. Cheese Dogs 43
53. Cheeseburger Patties................ 43
54. Chicken Cordon Bleu................ 44

SIDE DISHES 45

55. Buttered Corn 46
56. Bread Sticks 46
57. Polenta Sticks................ 47
58. Crispy Eggplant Slices 47
59. Simple Cauliflower Poppers 48
60. Crispy Cauliflower Poppers 48
61. Broccoli Poppers................ 49

62. Cheesy Broccoli Bites...49

63. Mixed Veggie Bites...50

64. Risotto Bites..50

65. Rice Flour Bites 51

66. Lemon Parmesan and Peas Risotto 51

67. Spinach and Goat Cheese Risotto 52

68. Rice and Artichokes 52

69. Potatoes Au Gratin 53

BEEF, LAMB & PORK RECIPES **54**

70. Cheeseburger Egg Rolls...55

71. Air Fried Grilled Steak 55

72. Juicy Cheeseburgers 56

73. Spicy Thai Beef Stir-Fry..56

74. Beef Brisket Recipe from Texas 57

75. Copycat Taco Bell Crunch Wraps.............................57

76. Steak and Mushroom Gravy 58

77. Air Fryer Beef Casserole 59

78. Meat Lovers' Pizza 60

79. Chimichurri Skirt Steak...61

80. Country Fried Steak...61

81. Creamy Burger & Potato Bake 62

82. Beefy 'n Cheesy Spanish Rice Casserole.....................62

83. Warming Winter Beef with Celery 63

84. Beef & Veggie Spring Rolls.......................................63

85. Asian Inspired Sichuan Lamb....................................64

86. Garlic and Rosemary Lamb Cutlets 65

87. Garlic Sauced Lamb Chops 65

88. Herb Encrusted Lamb Chops....................................66

89. Herbed Rack of Lamb..66

90. Lamb Roast with Root Vegetables 67

91. Lemon and Cumin Coated Rack of Lamb...................68

92. Macadamia Rack of Lamb 68

93. Perfect Lamb Burgers 69

94. Simple Yet Tasty Lamb Chops 70

95. Tandoori Lamb 70

96. Barbecue Flavored Pork Ribs 71

97. Rustic Pork Ribs..71

98. Italian Parmesan Breaded Pork Chops......................72

99. Crispy Breaded Pork Chops 72

100. Caramelized Pork Shoulder.....................................73

101. Roasted Pork Tenderloin 73

102. Bacon-Wrapped Pork Tenderloin 74

103. Dijon Garlic Pork Tenderloin 74

104. Pork Neck with Salad 75

105. Chinese Braised Pork Belly 75

106. Air Fryer Sweet and Sour Pork 76

107. Juicy Pork Ribs Ole 76

108. Teriyaki Pork Rolls..77

VEGETARIAN RECIPES **78**

109. Air Fryer Buffalo Cauliflower 79

110. Air Fryer Kale Chips 79

111. Air Fried Mozzarella Stalks 80

112. Air Fryer Vegan Fried Ravioli 81

113. Air Fryer Veg Pizza...82

114. Air Fryer Buffalo Cauliflower – Onion Dip 82

115. Air Fryer Low Sodium Baked Apple..........................83

116. Vegan Air Fryer Eggplant Parmesan Recipe 83

117. Vegan Cheese Samosa 84

118. Delicious Air Fryer Potato Chips 85

FISH AND SEAFOOD RECIPES **86**

119. Prawn Momo's Recipe 87

120. Fish Club Classic Sandwich.....................................87

121. Prawn Fried Baked Pastry 88

122. Fish Spicy Lemon Kebab 89

123. Fish Oregano Fingers 90

124. Prawn Grandma's Easy to Cook Wontons...............90

125. Tuna Sandwich 91

126. Salmon Tandoor...92

127. Carp Best Homemade Croquette............................93

128. Shrimp Momo's Recipe...93

129. Salmon Fries..94

130. Cheese Carp Fries..94

131. Oyster Club Sandwich 95

132. Lobster Grandma's Easy to Cook Wontons 95

133. Seafood Pizza 96

134. Crab Cakes 96

135. Cilantro-Lime Fried Shrimp 97

136. Salmon Croquettes 97

137. Beer-Battered Fish and Chips 98

138. Firecracker Shrimp 99

139. Coconut Shrimp 100

140. Spicy Shrimp Kebab 100

141. Lemon-Pepper Tilapia with Garlic Aioli 101

142. Blackened Shrimp 102

143. Fried Catfish Nuggets 102

144. Cornmeal Shrimp Po'boy 103

145. Crumbed Fish Fillets with Tarragon 104

146. Smoked and Creamed White Fish 104

147. Parmesan and Paprika Baked Tilapia 105

148. Tangy Cod Fillets 105

149. Fish and Cauliflower Cakes 106

POULTRY RECIPES 107

150. Honey and Wine Chicken Breasts 108

151. Crispy Honey Garlic Chicken Wings 108

152. Lemon-Pepper Chicken Wings 109

153. Cheesy Chicken in Leek-Tomato Sauce 109

154. Mexican Chicken Burgers 110

155. Fried Chicken Livers 110

156. Minty Chicken-Fried Pork Chops 111

157. Crispy Southern Fried Chicken 111

158. Tex-Mex Turkey Burgers 112

159. Air Fryer Turkey Breast 112

160. Mustard Chicken Tenders 113

161. Chicken Nuggets 113

162. Cheesy Chicken Fritters 114

163. Air Fryer Chicken Parmesan 114

164. Ricotta and Parsley Stuffed Turkey Breasts 115

APPETIZERS 116

165. Steamed Pot Stickers 117

166. Beef and Mango Skewers 117

167. Curried Sweet Potato Fries 118

168. Spicy Kale Chips with Yogurt Sauce 118

169. Phyllo Artichoke Triangles 119

170. Arancini 119

171. Pesto Bruschetta 120

172. Fried Tortellini with Spicy Dipping Sauce 120

173. Shrimp Toast 121

174. Bacon Tater Tots 121

175. Hash Brown Bruschetta 122

176. Waffle Fry Poutine 122

177. Crispy Beef Cubes 123

178. Buffalo Chicken Bites 123

179. Sweet and Hot Chicken Wings 124

PALEO RECIPES 125

180. Healthy Brussels Sprouts 126

181. Mediterranean Vegetables 126

182. Healthy Green Beans 127

183. Simple Tomatillo Salsa 127

184. Roasted Zucchini 127

185. Tasty Broccoli Bites 128

186. Healthy Apple Chips 128

187. Zucchini Chips 128

188. Roasted Eggplant 129

189. Kale Chips 129

190. Roasted Broccoli 130

191. Lemon Garlic Broccoli 130

192. Roasted Carrots 131

193. Garlic Herb Rib-Eye Steak 131

194. Tasty Beef Patties 132

DESSERT RECIPES 133

195. Angel Food Cake 134

196. Apple Pie in Air Fryer 134

197. Apple-Toffee Upside-Down Cake 135

198. Banana-Choco Brownies 135

199. Blueberry & Lemon Cake 136

200. Bread Pudding with Cranberry 136

201. Cherries 'n Almond Flour Bars 137

202. Cherry-Choco Bars 137

203. Chocolate Chip in a Mug 138

204. Choco-Peanut Mug Cake 138

205. Coco-Lime Bars 139

206. Coconut 'n Almond Fat Bombs............. 139

207. Coconutty Lemon Bars 140

208. Coffee 'n Blueberry Cake 140

209. Coffee Flavored Cookie Dough 141

CONCLUSION **143**

Introduction

The Smart Air Fryer Oven is a conducive way to cook appetizing healthy meals. Instead of cooking food in hot oil and fat that can affect your health, the machine uses fast, hot air to circulate and cook the food. This allows the outside of the food to be crisp and also ensures that the inner layers are cooked.

The fryer allows us to cook almost everything and many dishes. We can use the deep fryer for cooking meat, vegetables, poultry, fruits, fish, and a wide variety of desserts. You can prepare all your meals, from appetizers to main dishes, passing through desserts. Not to mention, the deep fryer also allows for homemade cans or even delicious cakes and pies.

How does the fryer work?

The innovation of the fryer is very easy and simple. Fried foods have a crisp texture because the hot oil heats the food quickly and equally on its surface. Oil is an excellent conductor of heat, which helps to cook all the ingredients quickly and simultaneously. For decades, chefs have used transfer ovens to mimic the effects of frying or cooking across the entire surface of the food. But the air never revolves fast enough to achieve this wonderful crunchy surface that we all enjoy in fried foods.

With this process, the air circulates in high degrees, up to 201 ° C, to "fry" any food such as chicken, fish, or chips, etc. This innovation has changed the whole idea of cooking by reducing fat by up to 80% compared to traditional fried fat.

Cooking the deep fryer releases heat through a heating element that cook's food in a healthier and more convenient way. There is also an exhaust fan just above the cooking chamber that provides the necessary airflow for the food. In this way, the food is prepared with constant hot air. This leads to the same heating temperature that reaches each part of the food that is cooked. Therefore, only the grill and exhaust fan helps the fryer to propel the air at a constant high speed to cook healthy food with less fat.

Internal pressure increases the temperature, which is then controlled by the exhaust system. The extractor fan also releases additional filtered air to cook food in a much healthier way. The deep fryer does not smell at all and is completely harmless, making it easy to use and environmentally friendly.

Benefits of the Deep Fryer:

- Healthier meals without oil.

- Eliminates kitchen odors using internal air filters.

- Facilitates cleaning due to lack of lubricating oils.

- Air Fryers can bake, broil and fry, providing more options.

- Can adjust and exit from most models and includes a digital timer.

The fryer is all-in-one that allows for quick and easy cooking. It also leads to many possibilities once you know it. Once you know the basics and become familiar with your fryer, you can experiment and modify the recipes in any way you prefer. You can prepare a large number of dishes in the fryer and customize your favorite oven to be compatible with the fryer. Everything comes in variety and many options, right?

Cooking perfect, delicious, and healthy meals has never been easier. You can see how this collection of recipes looks.

Enjoy!

Understanding Breville Smart Air Fryer Oven

1. Breville Smart Air Fryer Oven

The Breville Smart Fryer is one of the smart appliances for cooking. It looks like a transfer oven and also fries or cooks your food using the transfer method. The hot air revolves around the food placed on the cooking tray. The hot air circulation technology is the same as the transfer method. The heating elements are displayed on the top of the Breville Smart Deep Fryer with a full power fan. The fan helps to circulate the hot air flow evenly in the oven. This will allow you to cook your food quickly and evenly on all sides. Fry your food in much less oil. Take a tablespoon or less than a tablespoon of oil to fry and mash your food. If you want to fry a bowl of potato chips, your oven with the Breville Smart Air Fryer simply fries the potatoes in a tablespoon of oil. Makes your fries crisp on the outside and tender on the inside.

The Breville Smart Fryer is not only used to fry your food, but also to grill your favorite chicken, bake cakes and cookies, and also reheat your frozen foods. It comes with 13 smart cooking modes. These functions are toast, muffin, bake, broil, broil, pizza, cookies, warm, hot, potato, waterproof, dehydrated, and slow cook. It works with an intelligent Element IQ system that finds the cold spot and automatically adjusts the temperature with PID temperature sensing and digital control, giving you even and accurate cooking. Smart ovens automatically adjust the wattage of the heating elements to give you more flexibility when cooking. The smart fryer oven works with double speed transfer technology; With this technique, you can cook your food faster by reducing cooking time by transferring. The smart fryer comes with a display that shows the 11 smart functions, as well as the cooking temperature and time. The smart fryer is also equipped with a built-in oven light, you can turn this light on at any time to see the cooking progress, or it can turn on automatically after the cook cycle is complete.

The Smart Deep Fryer is made from the most durable materials. The oven shell is made of reinforced stainless steel. In the smart oven, quartz is used instead of the metallic element because the quartz responds faster compared to the metallic element. Heat your oven quickly and evenly. The interior of the smart oven is lined with a non-stick coating that makes your daily cleaning process easy. To avoid burns, the oven rack is a self-extracting magnetic shelf. When you open the oven door, the shelves are automatically removed in the middle of the oven.

The Breville Smart Oven Fryer has one of the most flexible cooking appliances that are easy for everyone to handle. It is more than just a toaster that functions as a deep fryer, working pot, slow cooker, and also has the ability to dehydrate food. If air frying alone is not your main goal, this is the right choice for your kitchen. This smart oven works very well to heat food to the right temperature thanks to the transfer technology. It is one of the more expensive toaster ovens in this section. If your priority is more function, good performance, and flexibility, then the *Breville Smart Oven Fryer* is the best choice for your family.

2. How to Prepare the Smart Oven Before the First Use

It is necessary to empty the smart oven for 20 minutes before the first use to remove any protective substance adhering to the elements. Before testing, first, place your oven in a well-ventilated area and follow the instructions below.

1. First, remove the advertising stickers, multiple covers, or any packing material from the oven.

2. Remove the baking sheet, crumb tray, dehydrator basket or skillet, pizza tray, baking sheet, broil rack, multi-pack rack, and wash in hot water or soapy water with a cloth smooth and pat dry.

3. Take a soft, damp sponge to clean the inside of the oven and dry it well.

4. Place your oven in a well-ventilated area, making sure it is at least 4-6 inches apart on both sides of the oven.

5. Now insert the crumb tray into the oven in place and plug the power cord into an electrical outlet.

6. The oven display will illuminate with an alarm sound, and the function menu will appear, and the default display is in the TOAST menu setting.

7. Now turn the SELECT/CONFIRM dial until the pointer reaches the PIZZA setting.

8. Press the START/STOP button. After pressing this button, the button's backlight glows red, and the digital oven display glows orange with an audible alert.

9. The display shows the heating flashing. After healing is complete, the oven alarms and timer automatically start measurements.

10. After completing the beeping oven cycle warning, turn off the START/STOP backlight, and the oven LCD display will turn white. This will indicate that the oven is ready for its first use.

3. Smart Oven Air Fryer Features

Breville smart air fryer comes with 13 smart cooking functions. These functions are as follows:

1. TOAST: This function is used to toast the bread. Makes your bread brown and crisp on the outside. It is also used for English muffins and frozen waffles.

2. BAGEL: This function is used to crisp the inside of the cut bun and also to make light toast on the outside. It is also ideal for baking thick slices of bread or potatoes.

3. ROAST: With this function, you can cook poultry, minced meat, fish, vegetables, and sausages. Also great for browning the tops of grits, pots, and desserts.

4. BAKE: This function is used for baking your favorite cakes, muffins, and brownies.

5. ROAST: With this function, you can cook your favorite meat and poultry. You can also cook a whole chicken. Baking makes food tender and juicy inside.

6. HEAT: This function helps prevent the growth of bacteria. Keeps your oven temperature 160 ° C / 70 ° C.

7. PIZZA: This feature melts the cheese topping and browns on the top during pizza slices.

8. TEST: With this function, you can create the ideal environment to test the dough, slices of bread, and pizza.

9. AIRFRY: With these functions, you can make your food crisp and golden. This function is ideal for French fries.

10. HEAT: This function is ideal for reheating frozen food or food scraps without browning or drying the food.

11. COOKIES: This function is used for baking your favorite cookies and other baked goods.

12. BUY COOKING: This function is used for cooking your food for a long time at low temperatures.

13. DEHYDRATATION: This function is used to dry food without heating or to cook it. It is ideal for dehydrating your favorite fruits.

4. Advantages of the Smart Air Fryer Oven

The smart fryer oven comes with several benefits, some of which are as follows:

Healthy and Fatty Foods

The smart fryer oven works with transfer technology. Blow hot air into the cooking pan to cook food quickly and evenly on all sides. When frying your food in a smart fryer, you need a tablespoon or less than a tablespoon of oil. One bowl of fries requires only one tablespoon of oil and makes the fries crisp on the outside and tender on the inside. If you are among the people who like fried food but are worried about extra calories, this kitchen appliance is for you.

Offers 13-in-1 Operation

The Breville smart air fryer oven offers 13 functions in one device. These functions are Toast, Bagel, Toast, Bake, Broil, Hot, Pizza, Proof, Air Fry, Reheat, Cookie, Slow Cook, and Dehydrate. These are all smart programs that offer flexible cooking.

Safe to Use

The smart fryer oven is one of the safest cooking appliances compared to a traditional one. While cooking your food, the appliance is closed on all sides; because of this, there is no risk of hot oil splashing on your finger. This is one of the safest frying methods compared to another traditional frying method. A narrow cooking method gives you a splatter-free cooking experience. Smart IQ technology makes the device safer, and there is no possibility of burning food. Smart IQ automatically detects and adjusts the temperature of the item according to the needs of the recipe.

Easy to Clean

The Breville smart fryer oven is made of reinforced stainless steel, and the inner body is coated with non-stick materials. All interior accessories are dishwasher safe. You can wash it in a dishwasher or also wash it with soapy water. The smart fryer cooks your food in much less oil. Less oil means less chaos.

5. Care and Cleaning

1. Before starting the cleaning process, ensure that the power cord has been unplugged. Allow your oven and accessories to cool to room temperature before beginning the cleaning process.

2. Clean the oven body with a soft, damp cleaning sponge during the cleaning process. When cleaning the glass door, you can use a glass cleaner and a plastic cleaning pad to clean. Do not use metal coatings that can scratch the surface of your oven.

3. The inner body of the oven consists of a non-stick coating. Use a soft, damp sponge to clean the inside of the oven. Apply detergent to a sponge and do not apply it directly to the body of the oven. You can also use a mild spray solution to avoid staining.

4. Before cleaning the components, make sure the oven has cooled down to room temperature and then wipe gently with a soft damp cloth or sponge.

5. Dust the crumb tray with a soft, damp sponge. You can use a non-abrasive liquid cleaner. Apply detergent to a sponge and clean the disc.

6. To clean a frying pan, immerse it in warm soapy water and wash it with the help of a plastic frying pan or a soft sponge.

7. Remember to always dry all accessories thoroughly before placing them in the oven. Put the crumb tray in place before plugging the oven into its socket. Now your oven is ready for the next use.

Breakfast Recipes

1. Basil Tomato Frittata

⏰ Prep Time 10 m | ⏱ Cooking Time 35 m | 6 Servings

Ingredients

- 12 eggs
- 1/2 cup cheddar cheese, grated
- 1 1/2 cups cherry tomatoes, cut in half
- 1/2 cup fresh basil, chopped
- 1 cup baby spinach, chopped
- 1/2 cup yogurt
- Pepper
- Salt

Directions

1. Spray a baking dish using cooking spray and set aside.
2. Insert wire rack in rack position 6. Select bake, set temperature 390 F, timer for 35 minutes. Press start to preheat the oven.
3. Whisk eggs and yogurt inside a large bowl.
4. Layer spinach, basil, tomatoes, and cheese in prepared baking dish. Pour egg mixture over spinach mixture. Season with pepper and salt.
5. Bake in the oven for 35 minutes.
6. Serve and enjoy.

Nutrition

Calories 188 | Fat 12.2 g | Carbohydrates 4.2 g | Sugar 3.4 g | Protein 15.2 g | Cholesterol 338 mg

2. Italian Breakfast Frittata

⏰ Prep Time 10 m | ⏱ Cooking Time 30 m | 4 Servings

Ingredients

- 8 eggs
- 1 tbsp. fresh parsley, chopped
- 3 tbsp. parmesan cheese, grated
- 2 small zucchinis, chopped and cooked
- 1/2 cup pancetta, chopped and cooked
- Pepper
- Salt

Directions

1. Spray a baking dish using cooking spray and set aside.
2. Insert wire rack in rack position 6. Select bake, set temperature 350 F, timer for 20 minutes. Press start to preheat the oven.
3. In a mixing bowl, whisk eggs with pepper and salt. Add parsley, cheese, zucchini, and pancetta and stir well.
4. Pour egg mixture into the baking dish that was prepared.
5. Bake frittata for 20 minutes.
6. Serve and enjoy.

Nutrition

Calories 327 | Fat 23.2 g | Carbohydrates 3.5 g | Sugar 1.7 g | Protein 26 g | Cholesterol 367 mg

3. Healthy Baked Omelette

⏰ Prep Time 10 m | ⏰ Cooking Time 45 m | 6 Servings

Ingredients

- 8 eggs
- 1 cup bell pepper, chopped
- 1/2 cup onion, chopped
- 1/2 cup cheddar cheese, shredded

- 6 oz. ham, diced and cooked
- 1 cup milk
- Pepper
- Salt

Directions

1. Spray an 8-inch baking dish using cooking spray and set aside.
2. Insert wire rack in rack position 6. Select bake, set temperature 350 F, timer for 45 minutes. Press start to preheat the oven.

3. In a large bowl, whisk milk with egg, pepper, and salt. Add remaining ingredients and stir well.
4. Pour egg mixture into the baking dish that was prepared.
5. Bake omelet for 45 minutes.
6. Slice and serve.

Nutrition

Calories 199 | Fat 12.3 g | Carbohydrates 6.1 g | Sugar 3.7 g | Protein 16.1 g | Cholesterol 248 mg

4. Easy Egg Casserole

⏰ Prep Time 10 m | ⏰ Cooking Time 55 m | 8 Servings

Ingredients

- 8 eggs
- 1/2 tsp garlic powder
- 2 cups cheddar cheese, shredded
- 1 cup milk
- 24 oz. frozen hash browns, thawed
- 1/2 onion, diced

- 1 red pepper, diced
- 4 bacon slices, diced
- 1/2 lb. turkey breakfast sausage
- Pepper
- Salt

Directions

1. Spray a 9*13-inch baking dish using cooking spray and set aside.
2. Insert wire rack in rack position 6. Select bake, set temperature 350 F, timer for 50 minutes. Press start to preheat the oven.
3. Cook the breakfast sausage in a pan over medium heat until cooked through. Drain well and set aside.
4. Cook bacon in the same pan. Drain well and keep aside.

5. In a mixing bowl, whisk eggs with milk, garlic powder, pepper, and salt. Add 1 cup cheese, hash browns, onion, red pepper, bacon, and sausage and stir well.
6. Pour the entire egg mixture into the baking dish. Sprinkle remaining cheese on top.
7. Cover dish with foil and bake for 50 minutes. Remove foil and bake for 5 more minutes.
8. Serve and enjoy.

Nutrition

Calories 479 | Fat 29.1 g | Carbohydrates 34.1 g | Sugar 4.2 g | Protein 20.2 g | Cholesterol 207 mg

5. Flavor Packed Breakfast Casserole

⏰ Prep Time 10 m | ⏰ Cooking Time 40 m | 8 Servings

Ingredients

- 12 eggs
- 1/2 cup cheddar cheese, shredded
- 1 tsp garlic powder
- 1 cup milk
- 1/4 cup onion, diced
- 2 bell pepper, cubed
- 4 small potatoes, cubed
- 2 cups sausage, cooked and diced
- Pepper
- Salt

Directions

1. Spray a 9*13-inch baking dish using cooking spray and keep aside.
2. Insert wire rack in rack position 6. Select bake, set temperature 350 F, timer for 40 minutes. Press start to preheat the oven.
3. In a large bowl, whisk eggs with milk, garlic powder, pepper, and salt.
4. Add sausage, bell peppers, and potatoes into the baking dish. Pour egg mixture over sausage mixture. Sprinkle with cheese and onion.
5. Bake casserole for 40 minutes.
6. Slice and serve.

Nutrition

Calories 232 | Fat 11.6 g | Carbohydrates 18.3 g | Sugar 4.6 g | Protein 14.2 g | Cholesterol 261 mg

6. Vegetable Sausage Egg Bake

⏰ Prep Time 10 m | ⏰ Cooking Time 35 m | 4 Servings

Ingredients

- 10 eggs
- 1 cup spinach, diced
- 1 cup onion, diced
- 1 cup pepper, diced
- 1 lb. sausage, cut into 1/2-inch pieces
- 1 tsp garlic powder
- 1/2 cup almond milk
- Pepper
- Salt

Directions

1. Spray an 8*8-inch baking dish with cooking spray and set aside.
2. Insert wire rack in rack position 6. Select bake, set temperature 390 F, timer for 35 minutes. Press start to preheat the oven.
3. In a bowl, whisk milk with eggs and spices. Add vegetables and sausage and stir to combine.
4. Pour the mixture of egg into the prepared baking dish. Bake for 35 minutes.
5. Slice and serve.

Nutrition

Calories 653 | Fat 50.6 g | Carbohydrates 12.6 g | Sugar 3.3 g | Protein 38.3 g | Cholesterol 504 mg

7. Cheese Broccoli Bake

⏱ Prep Time 10 m | ⏱ Cooking Time 30 m | 12 Servings

Ingredients

- 12 eggs
- 1 1/2 cup cheddar cheese, shredded
- 2 cups broccoli florets, chopped
- 1 small onion, diced
- 1 cup milk
- Pepper
- Salt

Directions

1. Spray a 9*13-inch baking dish using cooking spray and set aside.
2. Insert wire rack in rack position 6. Select bake, set temperature 390 F, timer for 30 minutes. Press start to preheat the oven.
3. In a large bowl, whisk eggs with milk, pepper, and salt. Add cheese, broccoli, and onion and stir well.
4. Pour the mixture of eggs into the prepared baking dish and bake for 30 minutes.
5. Slice and serve.

Nutrition

Calories 138 | Fat 9.5 g | Carbohydrates 3.1 g | Sugar 1.8 g | Protein 10.2 g | | Cholesterol 180 mg

8. Cheese Ham Omelette

⏱ Prep Time 10 m | ⏱ Cooking Time 25 m | 6 Servings

Ingredients

- 8 eggs
- 1 cup ham, chopped
- 1 cup cheddar cheese, shredded
- 1/3 cup milk
- Pepper
- Salt

Directions

1. Spray a 9*9-inch baking dish using cooking spray and set aside.
2. Insert wire rack in rack position 6. Select bake, set temperature 390 F, timer for 25 minutes. Press start to preheat the oven.
3. In a large bowl, whisk eggs with milk, pepper, and salt. Stir in ham and cheese.
4. Pour the mixture of eggs into the prepared baking dish and bake for 25 minutes.
5. Slice and serve.

Nutrition

Calories 203 | Fat 14.3 g | Carbohydrates 2.2 g | Sugar 1.2 g | Protein 16.3 g | Cholesterol 252 mg

9. Sweet Potato Frittata

Prep Time 10 m | Cooking Time 30 m | 6 Servings

Ingredients

- 10 eggs
- 1/4 cup goat cheese, crumbled
- 1 onion, diced
- 1 sweet potato, diced
- 2 cups broccoli, chopped
- 1 tbsp. olive oil
- Pepper
- Salt

Directions

1. Spray a baking dish using cooking spray and set aside.
2. Insert wire rack in rack position 6. Select bake, set temperature 390 F, timer for 20 minutes. Press start to preheat the oven.
3. Heat oil in a pan over medium heat. Add sweet potato, broccoli, and onion and cook for 10-15 minutes or until sweet potato is tender.
4. In a large bowl, whisk eggs with pepper and salt.
5. Transfer cooked vegetables into the baking dish. Pour egg mixture over vegetables. Spray in goat cheese and bake for 15-20 minutes.
6. Slice and serve.

Nutrition

Calories 201 | Fat 13 g | Carbohydrates 8.4 g | Sugar 3.3 g | Protein 13.5 g | Cholesterol 282 mg

10. Squash Oat Muffins

Prep Time 10 m | Cooking Time 20 m | 12 Servings

Ingredients

- 2 eggs
- 1 tbsp. pumpkin pie spice
- 2 tsp baking powder
- 1 cup oats
- 1 cup all-purpose flour
- 1 tsp vanilla
- 1/3 cup olive oil
- 1/2 cup yogurt
- 1/2 cup maple syrup
- 1 cup butternut squash puree
- 1/2 tsp sea salt

Directions

1. Line 12 cups muffin pan with cupcake liners.
2. Insert wire rack in rack position 6. Select bake, set temperature 390 F, timer for 20 minutes. Press start to preheat the oven.
3. In a large bowl, whisk together eggs, vanilla, oil, yogurt, maple syrup, and squash puree.
4. In a small bowl, mix together flour, pumpkin pie spice, baking powder, oats, and salt.
5. Add flour mixture into the moist mixture and stir to combine.
6. Scoop the batter to the prepared muffin pan and bake for 20 minutes.
7. Serve and enjoy.

Nutrition

Calories 171 | Fat 7.1 g | Carbohydrates 23.8 g | Sugar 9.4 g | Protein 3.6 g | Cholesterol 28 mg

11. Hashbrown Casserole

⏰ Prep Time 10 m | ⏱ Cooking Time 60 m | 10 Servings

Ingredients

- 2 cups cheddar cheese, shredded
- 15 eggs, lightly beaten
- 5 bacon slices, cooked and chopped
- 32 oz. frozen hash browns with onions and peppers
- Pepper
- Salt

Directions

1. Spray 9*13-inch casserole dish with cooking spray and set aside.
2. Insert wire rack in rack position 6. Select bake, set temperature 350 F, timer for 60 minutes. Press start to preheat the oven.
3. In a large bowl, whisk eggs with pepper and salt. Add 1 cup of cheese, bacon, and hash browns and mix well.
4. Pour egg mixture into the prepared casserole dish and sprinkle with remaining cheese.
5. Bake for 60 minutes or until the top is golden brown.
6. Slice and serve.

Nutrition

Calories 403 | Fat 27.1 g | Carbohydrates 23.6 g | Sugar 0.6 g | Protein 19 g | Cholesterol 280 mg

12. Mexican Breakfast Frittata

⏰ Prep Time 10 m | ⏱ Cooking Time 25 m | 6 Servings

Ingredients

- 8 eggs, scrambled
- 1/2 cup cheddar cheese, grated
- 3 scallions, chopped
- 1/3 lb. tomatoes, sliced
- 1 green pepper, chopped
- 1/2 cup salsa
- 2 tsp taco seasoning
- 1 tbsp. olive oil
- 1/2 lb. ground beef
- Pepper
- Salt

Directions

1. Spray a baking dish using cooking spray and set aside.
2. Insert wire rack in rack position 6. Select bake, set temperature 375 F, timer for 25 minutes. Press start to preheat the oven.
3. Heat oil in a pan over low heat. Add ground beef in a pan and cook until brown.
4. Add salsa, taco seasoning, scallions, and green pepper into the pan and stir well.
5. Transfer meat into the prepared baking dish. Arrange slices of tomato on top of the meat mixture.
6. In a bowl, whisk eggs with cheese, pepper, and salt. Pour egg mixture over the meat mixture and bake for 25 minutes.
7. Serve and enjoy.

Nutrition

Calories 231 | Fat 13.9 g | Carbohydrates 4.5 g | Sugar 2.5 g | Protein 22.2 g | Cholesterol 262 mg

13. Perfect Brunch Baked Eggs

⏱ Prep Time 10 m | ⏱ Cooking Time 20 m | 4 Servings

Ingredients

- 4 eggs
- 1/2 cup parmesan cheese, grated
- 2 cups marinara sauce
- Pepper
- Salt

Directions

1. Spray 4 shallow baking dishes using cooking spray and set aside.
2. Insert wire rack in rack position 6. Select bake, set temperature 390 F, timer for 20 minutes. Press start to preheat the oven.
3. Divide marinara sauce into four baking dishes.
4. Break the egg into each baking dish. Sprinkle cheese, pepper, and salt on top of eggs and bake for 20 minutes.
5. Serve and enjoy.

Nutrition

Calories 208 | Fat 10.1 g | Carbohydrates 18 g | Sugar 11.4 g | Protein 11.4 g | Cholesterol 174 mg

14. Green Chile Cheese Egg Casserole

⏱ Prep Time 10 m | ⏱ Cooking Time 40 m | 12 Servings

Ingredients

- 12 eggs
- 8 oz. can green chilies, diced
- 6 tbsp. butter, melted
- 3 cups cheddar cheese, shredded
- 2 cups curd cottage cheese
- 1 tsp baking powder
- 1/2 cup flour
- Pepper
- Salt

Directions

1. Spray a 9*13-inch baking dish using cooking spray and set aside.
2. Insert wire rack in rack position 6. Select bake, set temperature 350 F, timer for 40 minutes. Press start to preheat the oven.
3. In a large mixing bowl, beat eggs until fluffy. Add baking powder, flour, pepper, and salt.
4. Stir in green chilies, butter, cheddar cheese, and cottage cheese.
5. Pour the mixture of eggs into the prepared baking dish and bake for 40 minutes.
6. Slice and serve.

Nutrition

Calories 284 | Fat 21.3 g | Carbohydrates 7.4 g | Sugar 1.8 g | Protein 17 g | Cholesterol 217 mg

15. Breakfast Salmon Patties

⏰ Prep Time 10 m | ⏰ Cooking Time 8 m | 6 Servings

Ingredients

- 14 oz. can salmon, drained and minced
- 1 tsp paprika
- 2 tbsp. green onion, minced
- 2 tbsp. fresh coriander, chopped
- 1 egg, lightly beaten
- Pepper
- Salt

Directions

1. Preheat the instant vortex air fryer to 360 F.
2. Add all ingredients into the bowl and mix until well combined.
3. Spray air fryer oven pan with cooking spray.
4. Make six even shape patties from salmon mixture and place on pan and air fry for 6-8 minutes. Turn halfway through.
5. Serve and enjoy.

Nutrition

Calories 122 | Fat 5.6 g | Carbohydrates 0.4 g | Sugar 0.2 g | Protein 16.5 g | Cholesterol 56 mg

16. Zucchini Fries

⏰ Prep Time 10 m | ⏰ Cooking Time 10 m | 4 Servings

Ingredients

- 2 medium zucchini, cut into fries shape
- ½ tsp garlic powder
- 1 tsp Italian seasoning
- ½ cup parmesan cheese, grated
- ½ cup breadcrumbs
- 1 egg, lightly beaten
- Pepper
- Salt

Directions

1. In a shallow bowl, mix together parmesan cheese, breadcrumbs, Italian seasoning, garlic powder, pepper, and salt.
2. Coat zucchini pieces with egg then coat with breadcrumb mixture.
3. Spray air fryer oven tray with cooking spray.
4. Arrange coated zucchini fries on a tray and air fry at 400 F for 10 minutes.
5. Serve and enjoy.

Nutrition

Calories 240 | Fat 11.3 g | Carbohydrates 13.5 g | Sugar 2.8 g | Protein 16.5 g | Cholesterol 72 mg

17. Breakfast Stuffed Peppers

⏲ Prep Time 10 m | ⏲ Cooking Time 13 m | 2 Servings

Ingredients

- 4 eggs
- 1 bell pepper, halved and seed removed
- ¼ tsp red chili flakes
- Pepper
- Salt

Directions

1. Crack 2 eggs into each bell pepper half and season with pepper and salt.
2. Sprinkle red chili flakes on top.
3. Arrange peppers on air fryer oven tray and cook at 390 F for 13 minutes.
4. Serve and enjoy.

Nutrition

Calories 165 | Fat 11.2 g | Carbohydrates 5.2 g | Sugar 3.7 g | Protein 11.7 g | Cholesterol 327 mg

18. Crispy Breakfast Potatoes

⏲ Prep Time 10 m | ⏲ Cooking Time 20 m | 6 Servings

Ingredients

- 1 ½ lbs. potatoes, diced into ½-inch cubes
- 1 tsp paprika
- 1 tsp garlic powder
- 1 tbsp. olive oil
- ½ tbsp. dried parsley
- ¼ tsp chili powder
- ¼ tsp pepper
- 2 tsp salt

Directions

1. Add potatoes into the mixing bowl. Add remaining ingredients over the potatoes and toss until evenly coated.
2. Arrange potatoes on air fryer oven tray and air fry at 400 F for 20 minutes. Turn potatoes to the other side halfway through.
3. Serve and enjoy.

Nutrition

Calories 102 | Fat 2.5 g | Carbohydrates 18.5 g | Sugar 1.5 g | Protein 2.1 g | Cholesterol 0 mg

19. Quick Cheese Omelet

⏱ Prep Time 5 m | ⏱ Cooking Time 9 m | 1 Servings

Ingredients

- 2 eggs, lightly beaten
- ¼ cup cheddar cheese, shredded
- ¼ cup milk

- Pepper
- Salt

Directions

1. In a bowl, whisk milk, eggs with pepper, and salt.
2. Spray small air fryer pan with cooking spray.
3. Pour egg mixture into the prepared pan and cook at 350 F for 6 minutes.

4. Sprinkle cheese on top and cook for 3 minutes more.
5. Serve and enjoy.

Nutrition

Calories 270 | Fat 19.4 g | Carbohydrates 4.1 g | Sugar 3.6 g | Protein 20.1 g | Cholesterol 362 mg

20. Tomato Spinach Frittata

⏱ Prep Time 10 m | ⏱ Cooking Time 7 m | 1 Servings

Ingredients

- 2 eggs, lightly beaten
- ¼ cup spinach, chopped
- ¼ cup tomatoes, chopped
- 2 tbsp. milk

- 1 tbsp. parmesan cheese, grated
- Pepper
- Salt

Directions

1. In a medium bowl, whisk eggs. Add other ingredients and mix until well combined.
2. Spray small air fryer pan with cooking spray.

3. Pour egg mixture into the prepared pan and cook at 330 F for 7 minutes.
4. Serve and enjoy.

Nutrition

Calories 189 | Fat 11.7 g | Carbohydrates 4.3 g | Sugar 3.3 g | Protein 15.7 g | Cholesterol 337 mg

21. Ham Egg Brunch Bake

☺ Prep Time 10 m | ☺ Cooking Time 60 m | 6 Servings

Ingredients

- 4 eggs
- 20 oz. hash browns
- 1 onion, chopped
- 2 cups ham, chopped
- 3 cups cheddar cheese, shredded
- 1 cup sour cream
- 1 cup milk
- Pepper
- Salt

Directions

1. Spray a 9*13-inch baking dish using cooking spray and set aside.
2. Insert wire rack in rack position 6. Select bake, set temperature 375 F, timer for 35 minutes. Press start to preheat the oven.
3. In a large bowl, whisk eggs with sour cream, milk, pepper, and salt. Add 2 cups cheese and stir well.
4. Cook onion and ham in a medium pan until onion is softened.
5. Add hash brown to the pan and cook for 5 minutes.
6. Add onion ham mixture into the egg mixture and mix well.
7. Pour the mixture of eggs into the prepared baking dish. Cover dish with foil and bake for 35 minutes.
8. Remove foil and bake for 25 minutes more.
9. Slice and serve.

Nutrition

Calories 703 | Fat 46.2 g | Carbohydrates 41.2 g | Sugar 4.6 g | Protein 30.8 g | Cholesterol 214 mg

22. Roasted Brussels Sprouts & Sweet Potatoes

☺ Prep Time 10 m | ☺ Cooking Time 20 m | 4 Servings

Ingredients

- 1 lb. Brussels sprouts, cut in half
- 2 sweet potatoes, wash and cut into 1-inch pieces
- 2 tbsp. olive oil
- ¼ tsp garlic powder
- ½ tsp pepper
- 1 tsp salt

Directions

1. Add sweet potatoes and Brussels sprouts in the mixing bowl.
2. Add remaining ingredients over sweet potatoes and Brussels sprouts and toss until well coated.
3. Transfer sweet potatoes and Brussels sprouts on air fryer oven tray and roast at 400 F for 10 minutes.
4. Turn sweet potatoes and Brussels sprouts to the other side and roast for 10 minutes more.
5. Serve and enjoy.

Nutrition:

Calories 138 | Fat 7.4 g | Carbohydrates 17.2 g | Sugar 3.9 g | Protein 4.4 g | Cholesterol 0 mg

23. Roasted Potato Wedges

⏰ Prep Time 10 m | ⏰ Cooking Time 10 m | 6 Servings

Ingredients

- 2 lbs. potatoes, cut into wedges
- 2 tbsp. McCormick's chipotle seasoning
- ¼ cup olive oil

Directions

1. Add potato wedges into the mixing bowl.
2. Add remaining ingredients over potato wedges and toss until well coated.
3. Transfer potato wedges onto the air fryer oven tray roast at 400 F for 5 minutes.
4. Turn potato wedges to the other side and roast for 5 minutes more.
5. Serve and enjoy.

Nutrition

Calories 176 | Fat 8.6 g | Carbohydrates 23.8 g | Sugar 1.7 g | Protein 2.5 g | Cholesterol 0 mg

24. Breakfast Egg Bites

⏰ Prep Time 10 m | ⏰ Cooking Time 13 m | 4 Servings

Ingredients

- 4 eggs, lightly beaten
- ¼ cup ham, diced
- ¼ cup cheddar cheese, shredded
- ¼ cup bell pepper, diced
- ½ cup milk
- Pepper
- Salt

Directions

1. Add all necessary ingredients into the mixing bowl and whisk until well combined.
2. Spray muffin silicone mold with cooking spray.
3. Pour egg mixture into the silicone muffin mold and place it in the air fryer oven and bake at 350 F for 10 minutes.
4. After 10 minutes flip egg bites and cook for 3 minutes more.
5. Serve and enjoy.

Nutrition

Calories 123 | Fat 8.1 g | Carbohydrates 2.8 g | Sugar 2.1 g | Protein 9.8 g | Cholesterol 178 mg

25. Grilled Cheese Sandwich

⏰ Prep Time 5 m | ⏰ Cooking Time 4 m | 2 Servings

Ingredients

- 4 Texas toast slices

- 4 Colby jack cheese slices

Directions

1. Spray air fryer oven tray with cooking spray.

2. Place two toast slices on a tray then top with cheese slices.

3. Now place remaining toast slices on top of the cheese.

4. Air fry at 400 F for 4 minutes.

5. Serve and enjoy.

Nutrition

Calories 225 | Fat 4 g | Carbohydrates 38.5 g | Sugar 4 g | Protein 8.5 g | Cholesterol 5 mg

Main Recipes

26. Grilled Cheese Sandwich

⏱ Prep Time 5 m | ⏱ Cooking Time 5 m | 2 Servings

Ingredients

- 2 slices of bread, softened
- 1 tsp. butter

- 2 slices of cheddar cheese

Directions

1. Set the air fryer at a temperature of 350°F.
2. Apply 1/2 teaspoon of the softened butter to one side of the slice of bread. Repeat for the remaining bread.
3. Create the sandwich by putting the cheese in between the non-buttered sides of bread.

4. Transfer to the hot air fryer and set for 5 minutes. Flip the sandwich at the halfway point and remove it.
5. Serve immediately and enjoy it.

Nutrition

Calories 235 | Fat 13 g | Fiber 27 g| Carbs 37 g | Protein 40 g

27. Italian Meatballs

⏱ Prep Time 15 m | ⏱ Cooking Time 20 m | 4 Servings

Ingredients

- One egg, large
- Ground beef - 16 oz.
- Pepper - 1/8 tsp.
- Oregano seasoning - 1/2 tsp.
- Bread crumbs - 1 1/4 cup

- Garlic - 1/2 clove, chopped
- Parsley - 1 oz., chopped
- Salt - 1/4 tsp.
- Parmigiano-Reggiano cheese - 1 oz. cup, grated
- Cooking spray (avocado oil)

Directions

1. Whisk the oregano, breadcrumbs, chopped garlic, salt, chopped parsley, pepper, and grated Parmigiano-Reggiano cheese until combined.
2. Blend the ground beef and egg into the mixture using your hands. Incorporate the ingredients thoroughly.
3. Divide the meat into 12 sections and roll into rounds.

4. Coat the inside of the basket with avocado oil spray to grease.
5. Adjust the temperature to 350°F and heat for approximately 12 minutes.
6. Roll the meatballs over and steam for another 4 minutes and remove to a serving plate.
7. Enjoy as-is or combine with your favorite pasta or sauce.

Nutrition

Calories 321| Fat 3 g | Fiber 8 g | Carbs 22 g | Protein 16 g

28. Loaded Baked Potatoes

⏱ Prep Time 10 m | ⏱ Cooking Time 15 m | 3 Servings

Ingredients

- 1/3 cup milk
- 2 oz. sour cream
- 1/3 cup white cheddar, grated
- 2 oz. Parmesan cheese, grated
- 1/8 tsp. garlic salt

- 6 oz. ham, diced
- 2 medium russet potatoes
- 4 oz. sharp cheddar, shredded
- 1/8 cup. green onion, diced

Directions

1. Puncture the potatoes deeply with a fork a few times and microwave for approximately 5 minutes. Flip them to the other side and nuke for an additional 5 minutes. The potatoes should be soft.

2. Use oven mitts to remove from the microwave and cut them in halves.

3. Spoon out the insides of the potatoes to about a quarter-inch from the skins and distribute the potato flesh to a glass bowl.

4. Combine the parmesan, garlic salt, sour cream, and white cheddar cheese to the potato dish and incorporate fully.

5. Distribute the mixture back to the emptied potato skins. Create a small hollow in the middle by pressing with a spoon.

6. Divide the ham evenly between the potatoes and place the ham inside the hollow.

7. Position the potatoes in the fryer and set the air fryer to the temperature of 300°F.

8. Heat for 8 minutes and then sprinkle the cheddar cheese on top of each potato.

9. Melt the cheese for two more minutes than serve with diced onions on top.

Nutrition

Calories 143 | Fat 22 g | Fiber 14 g | Carbs 18 g | Protein 29 g

29. Pepperoni Pizza

⏰ Prep Time 5 m | ⏰ Cooking Time 5 m | 7 Servings

Ingredients

- 1 mini naan flatbread
- 2 tbsp. pizza sauce
- 7 slices mini pepperoni

- 1 tbsp. olive oil
- 2 tbsp. mozzarella cheese, shredded

Directions

1. Prepare the naan flatbread by brushed the olive oil on the top.
2. Layer the naan with pizza sauce, mozzarella cheese, and pepperoni.
3. Transfer to the frying basket and set the air fryer to the temperature of 375°F.
4. Heat for approximately 6 minutes and enjoy immediately.

Nutrition

Calories 430 | Fat 4 g | Fiber 9 g | Carbs 11 g | Protein 10 g

30. Southern Style Fried Chicken

⏰ Prep Time 10 m | ⏱ Cooking Time 15 m | 8 Servings

Ingredients

- Italian seasoning - 1 tsp.
- Chicken legs or breasts - 2 lbs.
- Buttermilk - 2 tbsp.
- Paprika seasoning - 1 1/2tsp.
- Cornstarch - 2 oz.
- Onion powder - 1 tsp.
- Hot sauce - 3 tsp.

- Pepper - 1 1/2 tsp.
- 2 large eggs
- 1 cup self-rising flour
- 2 tsp. salt
- Cooking spray (olive oil)
- 1/4 cup water
- Garlic powder - 1 1/2tsp.

Directions

1. Clean the chicken by washing thoroughly and pat dry with paper towels.
2. Use a glass dish to blend the pepper, paprika, garlic powder, onion powder, salt, and Italian seasoning.
3. Rub approximately 1 tablespoon of the spices into the pieces of chicken to cover entirely.
4. Blend the cornstarch, flour, and spices by shaking in a large ziplock bag.
5. In a separate dish, combine the eggs, hot sauce, water, and milk until integrated.
6. Completely cover the spiced chicken in the flour and then immerse in the eggs.
7. Coat in the flour for a second time and set on a tray for approximately 15 minutes.
8. Before transferring the chicken to the air fryer, spray liberally with olive oil and space the pieces out, frying a separate batch if required.
9. Adjust the temperature to 350° F for approximately 18 minutes.
10. Bring the chicken out and put on a plate. Wait about 5 minutes before serving.

Nutrition

Calories 230 | Fat 10 g | Fiber 19 g | Carbs 13 g | Protein 12 g

31. Stuffed Bell Peppers

⏱ Prep Time 15 m | ⏱ Cooking Time 15 m | 9 Servings

Ingredients

- Medium onion - 1/2, chopped
- Cheddar cheese - 4 oz., shredded
- Pepper - 1/2 tsp.
- Ground beef - 8 oz.
- Olive oil - 1 tsp.
- Tomato sauce - 4 oz.

- Worcestershire sauce - 1 tsp.
- Medium green peppers - 2, stems and seeds discarded
- Salt - 1 tsp., separated
- Water - 4 cups
- Garlic - 1 clove, minced

Directions

1. Boil the water in pot steam the green peppers with the tops and seeds removed with 1/2 teaspoon of the salt. Move from the burner after approximately 3 minutes and drain.

2. Pat the peppers with paper towels to properly dry.

3. In a hot frying pan, melt the olive oil and toss the garlic and onion for approximately 2 minutes until browned. Drain thoroughly.

4. Set the air fryer temperature to 400°F to warm up.

5. Using a glass dish, blend the beef along with Worcestershire sauce, 2 ounces of tomato sauce, salt, vegetables, 2 ounces of cheddar cheese, and pepper until fully incorporated.

6. Spoon the mixture evenly into the peppers and drizzle the remaining 2 ounces of tomato sauce on top. Then dust with the remaining 2 ounces of cheddar cheese.

7. Assemble the peppers in the basket of the air fryer and heat fully for approximately 18 minutes. The meat should be fully cooked before removing it.

8. Place on a platter and serve immediately.

Nutrition

Calories 120 | Fat 9 g | Fiber 2 g | Carbs 17 g | Protein 28 g

32. Tuna Patties

⏰ Prep Time 5 m | ⏰ Cooking Time 15 m | 2 Servings

Ingredients

- Garlic powder - 1 tsp.
- Tuna - 2 cans, in water
- Dill seasoning - 1 tsp.
- All-purpose flour - 4 tsp.
- Salt - 1/4 tsp.
- Mayonnaise - 4 tsp.
- Lemon juice - 2 tbsp.
- Onion powder - 1/2 tsp.
- Pepper - 1/4 tsp.

Directions

1. Set the temperature of the air fryer to 400°F.
2. Combine the almond flour, mayonnaise, salt, onion powder, dill, garlic powder, and pepper using a food blender for approximately 30 seconds until incorporated.
3. Empty the canned tuna and lemon juice into the blender and pulse for an additional 30 seconds until integrated fully.
4. Divide evenly into 4 sections and create patties by hand.
5. Transfer to the fryer basket in a single layer and heat for approximately 12 minutes.

Nutrition

Calories 286 | Fat 3 g | Fiber 6 g | Carbs 22 g | Protein 16 g

33. Ham and Cheese Sandwich

⏰ Prep Time 15 m | ⏰ Cooking Time 20 m | 2 Servings

Ingredients

- 2 eggs
- 4 slices of bread of choice
- 4 slices turkey
- 4 slices ham
- 6 tbsp. half and half cream
- 2 tsp. melted butter
- 4 slices Swiss cheese
- ¼ tsp. pure vanilla extract
- Powdered sugar and raspberry jam for serving

Directions

1. Mix the eggs, vanilla, and cream in a bowl and set aside.
2. Make a sandwich with the bread layered with cheese slice, turkey, ham, cheese slice, and the top slice of bread to make two sandwiches. Gently press on the sandwiches to somewhat flatten them.
3. Set your air fryer toast oven to 350 degrees F.
4. Spread out kitchen aluminum foil and cut it about the same size as the sandwich and spread the melted butter on the surface of the foil.
5. Dip the sandwich in the egg mixture and let it soak for about 20 seconds on each side. Repeat this for the other sandwich. Place the soaked sandwiches on the prepared foil sheets then place them on the basket in your fryer.
6. Cook for 12 minutes then flip the sandwiches and brush with the remaining butter and cook for another 5 minutes or until well browned.
7. Place the sandwich on a plate and top with the powdered sugar and serve with a small bowl of raspberry jam.

Nutrition

Calories 170 | Fat 22 g | Fiber 10 g | Carbs 12 g | Protein 20 g

34. Easy Hot Dogs

⏰ Prep Time 10 m | ⏱ Cooking Time 7 m | 2 Servings

Ingredients

- 2 hot dog buns
- 2 hot dogs
- 1 tablespoon Dijon mustard
- 2 tablespoons cheddar cheese, grated

Directions

1. Put hot dogs in the preheated air fryer and cook them at 390 degrees F for 5 minutes.

2. Divide hot dogs into hot dog buns, spread mustard and cheese, return everything to your air fryer and cook for 2 minutes more at 390 degrees F.

3. Serve for lunch. Enjoy!

Nutrition:

Calories 211 | Fat 3 g | Fiber 8 g | Carbs 12 g | Protein 4 g

35. Japanese Chicken Mix

⏰ Prep Time 10 m | ⏱ Cooking Time 8 m | 2 Servings

Ingredients

- 2 chicken thighs, skinless and boneless
- 2 ginger slices, chopped
- 3 garlic cloves, minced
- ¼ cup soy sauce
- ¼ cup mirin
- 1/8 cup sake
- ½ teaspoon sesame oil
- 1/8 cup water
- 2 tablespoons sugar
- 1 tablespoon cornstarch mixed with 2 tablespoons water
- Sesame seeds for serving

Directions

1. In a bowl, mix chicken thighs with ginger, garlic, soy sauce, mirin, sake, oil, water, sugar, and cornstarch, toss well, transfer to preheated air fryer and cook at 360 degrees F for 8 minutes.

2. Divide among plates, sprinkle sesame seeds on top and serve with a side salad for lunch.

Nutrition

Calories 300 | Fat 7 g | Fiber 9 g | Carbs 17 g | Protein 10 g

36. Prosciutto Sandwich

⏱ Prep Time 10 m | ⏱ Cooking Time 5 m | 1 Servings

Ingredients

- 2 bread slices
- 2 mozzarella slices
- 2 tomato slices
- 2 prosciutto slices
- 2 basil leaves
- 1 teaspoon olive oil
- A pinch of salt and black pepper

Directions

1. Arrange mozzarella and prosciutto on a bread slice.
2. Season with salt and pepper, place in your air fryer and cook at 400 degrees F for 5 minutes.
3. Drizzle oil over prosciutto, add tomato and basil, cover with the other bread slice, cut the sandwich in half, and serve.

Nutrition

Calories 172 | Fat 3 g | Fiber 7 g | Carbs 9 g | Protein 5

37. Lentils Fritters

⏱ Prep Time 10 m | ⏱ Cooking Time 10 m | 2 Servings

Ingredients

- 1 cup yellow lentils, soaked in water for 1 hour and drained
- 1 hot chili pepper, chopped
- 1-inch ginger piece, grated
- ½ teaspoon turmeric powder
- 1 teaspoon garam masala
- 1 teaspoon baking powder
- Salt and black pepper to the taste
- 2 teaspoons olive oil
- 1/3 cup water
- ½ cup cilantro, chopped
- 1 and ½ cup spinach, chopped
- 4 garlic cloves, minced
- ¾ cup red onion, chopped
- Mint chutney for serving

Directions

1. In your blender, mix lentils with chili pepper, ginger, turmeric, garam masala, baking powder, salt, pepper, olive oil, water, cilantro, spinach, onion, and garlic, blend well and shape medium balls out of this mix.
2. Place them all in your preheated air fryer at 400 degrees F and cook for 10 minutes.
3. Serve your veggie fritters with a side salad for lunch.

Nutrition:

Calories 142 | Fat 2 g | Fiber 8 g | Carbs 12 g | Protein 4 g

38. Lunch Potato Salad

⏰ Prep Time 10 m | ⏰ Cooking Time 25 m | 4 Servings

Ingredients

- 2-pound red potatoes, halved
- 2 tablespoons olive oil
- Salt and black pepper to the taste
- 2 green onions, chopped
- 1 red bell pepper, chopped
- 1/3 cup lemon juice
- 3 tablespoons mustard

Directions

1. On your air fryer's basket, mix potatoes with half of the olive oil, salt, and pepper and cook at 350 degrees F for 25 minutes shaking the fryer once.
2. In a bowl, mix onions with bell pepper and roasted potatoes and toss.
3. In a small bowl, mix lemon juice with the rest of the oil and mustard and whisk really well.
4. Add this to potato salad, toss well and serve for lunch.

Nutrition

Calories 211 | Fat 6 g | Fiber 8 g | Carbs 12 g | Protein 4 g

39. Corn Casserole

⏰ Prep Time 10 m | ⏰ Cooking Time 15 m | 4 Servings

Ingredients

- 2 cups corn
- 3 tablespoons flour
- 1 egg
- ¼ cup milk
- ½ cup light cream
- ½ cup Swiss cheese, grated
- 2 tablespoons butter
- Salt and black pepper to the taste
- Cooking spray

Directions

1. In a bowl, mix the corn with flour, egg, milk, light cream, cheese, salt, pepper, and butter and stir well.
2. Grease your air fryer's pan with cooking spray, pour the cream mix, spread, and cook at 320 degrees F for 15 minutes.
3. Serve warm for lunch.

Nutrition:

Calories 281 | Fat 7 g | Fiber 8 g | Carbs 9 g | Protein 6 g

40. Bacon and Garlic Pizzas

⏰ Prep Time 10 m | ⏲ Cooking Time 10 m | 4 Servings

Ingredients

- 4 dinner rolls, frozen
- 4 garlic cloves minced
- ½ teaspoon oregano dried
- ½ teaspoon garlic powder

- 1 cup tomato sauce
- 8 bacon slices, cooked and chopped
- 1 and ¼ cups cheddar cheese, grated
- Cooking spray

Directions

1. Place dinner rolls on a working surface and press them to obtain 4 ovals.
2. Spray each oval with cooking spray, transfer them to your air fryer and cook them at 370 degrees F for 2 minutes.

3. Spread tomato sauce on each oval, divide garlic, sprinkle oregano, and garlic powder, and top with bacon and cheese.
4. Return pizzas to your heated air fryer and cook them at 370 degrees F for 8 minutes more.
5. Serve them warm for lunch.

Nutrition

Calories 217 | Fat 5 g | Fiber 8 g | Carbs 12 g | Protein 4 g

41. Sweet and Sour Sausage Mix

⏰ Prep Time 10 m | ⏲ Cooking Time 10 m | 4 Servings

Ingredients

- 1 pound sausages, sliced
- 1 red bell pepper, cut into strips
- ½ cup yellow onion, chopped
- 3 tablespoons brown sugar

- 1/3 cup ketchup
- 2 tablespoons mustard
- 2 tablespoons apple cider vinegar
- ½ cup chicken stock

Directions

1. In a bowl, mix sugar with ketchup, mustard, stock, and vinegar and whisk well.

2. In your air fryer's pan, mix sausage slices with bell pepper, onion, and sweet and sour mix, toss and cook at 350 degrees F for 10 minutes.
3. Divide into bowls and serve for lunch.

Nutrition

Calories 162 | Fat 6 g | Fiber 9 g | Carbs 12 g | Protein 6 g

42. Meatballs and Tomato Sauce

⏰ Prep Time 10 m | ⏰ Cooking Time 15 m | 4 Servings

Ingredients

- 1 pound lean beef, ground
- 3 green onions, chopped
- 2 garlic cloves, minced
- 1 egg yolk
- ¼ cup bread crumbs
- Salt and black pepper to the taste
- 1 tablespoon olive oil
- 16 ounces' tomato sauce
- 2 tablespoons mustard

Directions

1. In a bowl, mix beef with onion, garlic, egg yolk, bread crumbs, salt, and pepper, stir well, and shape medium meatballs out of this mix.
2. Grease meatballs with the oil, place them in your air fryer, and cook them at 400 degrees F for 10 minutes.
3. In a bowl, mix tomato sauce with mustard, whisk, add over meatballs, toss them and cook at 400 degrees F for 5 minutes more.
4. Divide meatballs and sauce among plates and serve for lunch.

Nutrition

Calories 300 | Fat 8 g | Fiber 9 g | Carbs 16 g | Protein 5 g

43. Stuffed Meatballs

⏰ Prep Time 10 m | ⏰ Cooking Time 10 m | 4 Servings

Ingredients

- 1/3 cup bread crumbs
- 3 tablespoons milk
- 1 tablespoon ketchup
- 1 egg
- ½ teaspoon marjoram, dried
- Salt and black pepper to the taste
- 1 pound lean beef, ground
- 20 cheddar cheese cubes
- 1 tablespoon olive oil

Directions

1. In a bowl, mix bread crumbs with ketchup, milk, marjoram, salt, pepper, and the egg and whisk well.
2. Add beef, stir and shape 20 meatballs out of this mix.
3. Shape each meatball around a cheese cube, drizzle the oil over them and rub.
4. Place all meatballs in your preheated air fryer and cook at 390 degrees F for 10 minutes.
5. Serve them for lunch with a side salad.

Nutrition

Calories 200 | Fat 5 g | Fiber 8 g | Carbs 12 g | Protein 5 g

44. Steaks and Cabbage

⏰ Prep Time 10 m | ⏰ Cooking Time 10 m | 4 Servings

Ingredients

- ½ pound sirloin steak, cut into strips
- 2 teaspoons cornstarch
- 1 tablespoon peanut oil
- 2 cups green cabbage, chopped
- 1 yellow bell pepper, chopped
- 2 green onions, chopped
- 2 garlic cloves, minced
- Salt and black pepper to the taste

Directions

1. In a bowl, mix cabbage with salt, pepper, and peanut oil, toss, transfer to air fryer's basket, cook at 370 degrees F for 4 minutes and transfer to a bowl.

2. Add steak strips to your air fryer, also add green onions, bell pepper, garlic, salt and pepper, toss, and cook for 5 minutes.

3. Add over cabbage, toss, divide among plates, and serve for lunch. Enjoy!

Nutrition

Calories 282 | Fat 6 g | Fiber 8 g | Carbs 14 g | Protein 6 g

45. Succulent Lunch Turkey Breast

⏰ Prep Time 10 m | ⏰ Cooking Time 47 m | 4 Servings

Ingredients

- 1 big turkey breast
- 2 teaspoons olive oil
- ½ teaspoon smoked paprika
- 1 teaspoon thyme, dried
- ½ teaspoon sage, dried
- Salt and black pepper to the taste
- 2 tablespoons mustard
- ¼ cup maple syrup
- 1 tablespoon butter, soft

Directions

1. Brush turkey breast with olive oil, season with salt, pepper, thyme, paprika, and sage. Rub, place in your air fryer's basket and fry at 350 degrees F for 25 minutes.

2. Flip turkey, cook for 10 minutes more, flip one more time, and cook for another 10 minutes.

3. Meanwhile, heat up a pan with the butter over medium heat, add mustard and maple syrup, stir well, cook for a couple of minutes and take off the heat.

4. Slice the turkey breast, divide among plates and serve with the maple glaze drizzled on top.

Nutrition

Calories 280 | Fat 2 g | Fiber 7 g | Carbs 16 g | Protein 14 g

46. Italian Eggplant Sandwich

⏰ Prep Time 10 m | ⏲ Cooking Time 16 m | 2 Servings

Ingredients

- 1 eggplant, sliced
- 2 teaspoons parsley, dried
- Salt and black pepper to the taste
- ½ cup breadcrumbs
- ½ teaspoon Italian seasoning
- ½ teaspoon garlic powder
- ½ teaspoon onion powder
- 2 tablespoons milk
- 4 bread slices
- Cooking spray
- ½ cup mayonnaise
- ¾ cup tomato sauce
- 2 cups mozzarella cheese, grated

Directions

1. Season eggplant slices with salt and pepper, leave aside for 10 minutes, and then pat dry them well.
2. In a bowl, mix parsley with breadcrumbs, Italian seasoning, onion and garlic powder, salt and black pepper and stir.
3. In another bowl, mix milk with mayo and whisk well.
4. Brush eggplant slices with mayo mix, dip them in breadcrumbs, place them in your air fryer's basket, spray with cooking oil and cook them at 400 degrees F for 15 minutes, flipping them after 8 minutes.
5. Brush each bread slice with olive oil and arrange 2 on a working surface.
6. Add mozzarella and parmesan on each, add baked eggplant slices, spread tomato sauce and basil and top with the other bread slices, greased side down.
7. Divide sandwiches among plates, cut them in halves, and serve for lunch.

Nutrition

Calories 324 | Fat 16 g | Fiber 4 g | Carbs 39 g | Protein 12 g

47. Creamy Chicken Stew

⏰ Prep Time 10 m | ⏲ Cooking Time 25 m | 4 Servings

Ingredients

- 1 and ½ cups canned cream of celery soup
- 6 chicken tenders
- Salt and black pepper to the taste
- 2 potatoes, chopped
- 1 bay leaf
- 1 thyme spring, chopped
- 1 tablespoon milk
- 1 egg yolk
- ½ cup heavy cream

Directions

1. In a bowl, mix chicken with cream of celery, potatoes, heavy cream, bay leaf, thyme, salt and pepper, toss, pour into your air fryer's pan, and cook at 320 degrees F for 25 minutes.
2. Leave your stew to cool down a bit, discard bay leaf, divide among plates, and serve right away.

Nutrition

Calories 300 | Fat 11 g | Fiber 2 g | Carbs 23 g | Protein 14 g

48. Lunch Pork and Potatoes

⏰ Prep Time 10 m | ⏱ Cooking Time 25 m | 2 Servings

Ingredients

- 2 pounds' pork loin
- Salt and black pepper to the taste
- 2 red potatoes, cut into medium wedges
- ½ teaspoon garlic powder
- ½ teaspoon red pepper flakes
- 1 teaspoon parsley, dried
- A drizzle of balsamic vinegar

Directions

1. In your air fryer's pan, mix pork with potatoes, salt, pepper, garlic powder, pepper flakes, parsley, and vinegar, toss and cook at 390 degrees F for 25 minutes.

2. Slice pork, divide it, divide the potatoes among plates, and serve for lunch.

Nutrition

Calories 400 | Fat 15 g | Fiber 7 g | Carbs 27 g | Protein 20 g

49. Bacon Cheddar Chicken Fingers

⏱ Prep Time 8 m | ⏱ Cooking Time 12 m | 8 Servings

Ingredients

For the chicken fingers:

- 1 lb. chicken tenders, about 8 pieces
- Cooking spray (canola oil)
- Cheddar cheese - 1 cup, shredded
- Two eggs, large
- 1/3 cup bacon bits
- 2 tbsp. water

For the breading:

- 1 tsp. of onion powder
- Panko bread crumbs - 2 cups
- Black pepper - 1 tsp., freshly ground
- Paprika - 2 tbsp.
- Garlic powder - 1 tsp.
- Salt - 2 tsp.

Directions

1. Set the air fryer to the temperature of 360°F.
2. In a glass dish, whip the water and eggs until combined.
3. Use a zip lock bag, shake the garlic powder, salt, breadcrumbs, cayenne, onion powder, and pepper together.
4. Immerse the chicken into the eggs and shake in the ziplock bag until fully covered.
5. Dip again in the mixture of egg and back into the seasonings until a thick coating is present.
6. Remove the tenders from the bag and set in the frying pan in the basket. Do them in batches if you need to not overpack the pan.
7. Apply the canola oil spray to the top of the tenders and heat for 6 minutes.
8. Flip the tenders to the other side. Steam for another 4 m.
9. Blend the bacon bits and shredded cheese in a dish.
10. Evenly dust the bacon and cheese onto the hot tenders and fry for 2 more minutes.
11. Remove and serve while hot.

Nutrition:

Calories 320 | Fat 25 g | Fiber 17 g | Carbs 37 g | Protein 40 g

50. Battered Cod

⏱ Prep Time 16 m | ⏱ Cooking Time 14 m | 2 Servings

Ingredients

- Cod - 20 oz.
- Salt - 1/4 tsp.
- All-purpose flour - 8 oz.
- Parsley seasoning - 1 tbsp.
- Cornstarch - 3 tsp.
- Garlic powder - 1/2 tsp.
- Two eggs, preferably large
- Onion powder - 1/2 tsp.

Directions

1. Whip the eggs in a glass dish until smooth and set to the side.
2. In a separate dish, blend the cornstarch, salt, almond flour, garlic powder, parsley, and onion powder, whisking to remove any lumpiness.
3. Immerse the pieces of cod into the egg and then into the spiced flour, covering completely.
4. Transfer to the fryer basket in a single layer.
5. Heat the fish for 7 minutes at a temperature of 350°F. Turn the cod over and steam for an additional 7 minutes.

Nutrition

Calories 254 | Fat 4 g | Fiber 10 g | Carbs 17 g | Protein 12 g

51. Beef Kabobs

⏱ Prep Time 10 m | ⏱ Cooking Time 12 m | 3 Servings

Ingredients

- Low-fat sour cream - 1/3 cup
- One bell pepper
- 16 oz. of beef chuck ribs, boneless
- Soy sauce - 2 tbsp.
- 6-inch skewers - 8
- Pepper - 1/4 tsp.
- Medium onion - 1/2

Directions

1. Slice the ribs into sections about 1-inch wide
2. In a lidded tub, combine the soy sauce, ribs, and sour cream, making sure the meat is fully covered.
3. Refrigerate for half an hour, at least, if not overnight.
4. Immerse the wooden skewers for approximately 10 minutes in water.
5. Set the temperature of the air fryer oven to 400°F.
6. Slice the onion and bell pepper in 1-inch sections.
7. Remove the meat from the marinade, draining well.
8. Layer the onions, beef, and bell peppers on the skewers and dust with pepper.
9. Heat for 10 minutes, ensuring you spin the skewers 5 minutes into cooking time.
10. Serve while hot and enjoy.

Nutrition

Calories 312 | Fat 10 g | Fiber 8 g | Carbs 29 g | Protein 30 g

52. Cheese Dogs

⏰ Prep Time 3 m | ⏰ Cooking Time 10 m | 7 Servings

Ingredients

- 4 hotdogs
- 1/4 cup your choice of cheese, grated
- 4 hotdog buns

Directions

1. Adjust the air fryer to heat at a temperature of 390°F for approximately 5 minutes.
2. Set the hot dogs in the basket and broil for 5 minutes.
3. Remove and create the hot dog with the bun and cheese as desired and move back to the basket for another 2 minutes.
4. Remove and enjoy while hot.

Nutrition

Calories 200 | Fat 5 g | Fiber 10 g | Carbs 17 g | Protein 18 g

53. Cheeseburger Patties

⏰ Prep Time 10 m | ⏰ Cooking Time 13 m | 4 Servings

Ingredients

- Garlic - 1/2 clove, minced
- Ground beef - 1 1/3 cup
- Onion - 4 oz., diced
- Worcestershire sauce - 2 tbsp.
- One egg, large
- Panko breadcrumbs - 2 oz.
- Cayenne pepper - 1/8 tsp.
- Cooking spray (olive oil)
- Salt - 1/4 tsp.
- 4 slices of cheese of your choice
- 1/8 tsp. pepper

Directions

1. Using a big glass dish, combine the diced onion, pepper, minced garlic, cayenne pepper, breadcrumbs, and salt until incorporated.
2. Blend the ground beef, Worcestershire sauce, and egg and integrate thoroughly by hand.
3. Form the meat into 4 individual patties and move to the air fryer basket.
4. Coat the patties with cooking spray.
5. Adjust the temperature for 375°F and heat for 8 minutes.
6. Turn the burgers over and steam for an additional 2 minutes.
7. Cover with a slice of cheese and continue cooking for approximately 3 minutes.
8. Enjoy or place on a bun with your favorite toppings.

Nutrition

Calories 287 | Fat 6 g | Fiber 12 g | Carbs 11 g | Protein 21 g

54. Chicken Cordon Bleu

⏱ Prep Time 15 m | ⏱ Cooking Time 20 m | 2 Servings

Ingredients

- Pepper - 1/4 tsp.
- Chicken paillards - 4
- Salt - 1/4 tsp.
- Swiss cheese - 8 slices
- All-purpose flour - 1/2 cup
- Parmesan cheese - 2/3 cup, grated

- Panko breadcrumbs - 1 1/2 cup
- Ham - 8 slices
- Two eggs, large
- Dijon mustard - 2 tbsp.
- 8 toothpicks
- Grapeseed oil spray

Directions

1. On a section of baking lining, brush the Dijon mustard on each chicken paillard and sprinkle with pepper and salt.
2. Layer 1 cheese, 2 slices of the ham, and then the additional slice of cheese on each of the pieces of chicken.
3. Rotate the chicken beginning with the longer side to create a roll. Fasten in place with two toothpicks.
4. Whip the egg in one dish, empty the flour into a second dish and blend the parmesan cheese and breadcrumbs into a third.
5. Immerse one chicken first in flour, secondly immerse in the egg and then roll the chicken completely in the breadcrumbs. Press the cheese and breadcrumbs into the chicken to secure and place onto a plate.
6. Repeat for the other pieces of chicken.
7. Apply the grapeseed oil spray to each section of chicken and transfer to the air fryer basket after 5 minutes.
8. Set the air fryer temperature to heat at 350°.
9. Grill for 8 minutes and carefully turn the chicken to the other side—heat for an additional 8 minutes.
10. Remove to a serving dish and wait approximately 5 minutes before serving hot.

Nutrition

Calories 176 | Fat 22 g | Fiber 20 g | Carbs 33 g | Protein 12 g

Side Dishes

55. Buttered Corn

⏰ Prep Time 5 m | ⏰ Cooking Time 20 m | 2 Servings

Ingredients

- 2 corn on the cob
- Salt and freshly ground black pepper, as needed
- 2 tablespoons butter, softened and divided

Directions

1. Sprinkle the cobs evenly with salt and black pepper.
2. Then, rub with 1 tablespoon of butter.
3. With 1 piece of foil, wrap each cob.
4. Press the "Power Button" of Air Fry Oven and turn the dial to select the "Air Fry" mode.
5. Press the Time button and again turn the dial to set the cooking time to 20 minutes.
6. Now push the Temp button and rotate the dial to set the temperature at 320 degrees F.
7. Press the "Start/Pause" button to start.
8. When the unit beeps to show that it is preheated, open the lid.
9. Arrange the cobs in "Air Fry Basket" and insert them in the oven.
10. Serve warm.

Nutrition

Calories 186 | Fat 12.2g | Saturated Fat 7.4g | Cholesterol 31mg | Sodium 163mg | Carbs 20.1g | Fiber 2.5g | Sugar 3.2g | Protein 2.9g

56. Bread Sticks

⏰ Prep Time 15 m | ⏰ Cooking Time 6 m | 6 Servings

Ingredients

- 1 egg 1/8 teaspoon ground cinnamon
- Salt, to taste
- 2 bread slices
- Pinch of nutmeg Pinch of ground cloves
- 1 tablespoon butter, softened
- Nonstick cooking spray
- 1 tablespoon icing sugar

Directions

1. In a bowl, add the eggs, cinnamon, nutmeg, cloves, and salt and beat until well combined.
2. Spread the butter over both sides of the slices evenly.
3. Cut each bread slice into strips.
4. Dip bread strips into egg mixture evenly.
5. Press the "Power Button" of Air Fry Oven and turn the dial to select the "Air Fry" mode.
6. Press the Time button and again turn the dial to set the cooking time to 6 minutes.
7. Now push the Temp button and rotate the dial to set the temperature at 355 degrees F.
8. Press the "Start/Pause" button to start.
9. When the unit beeps to show that it is preheated, open the lid.
10. Arrange the breadsticks in "Air Fry Basket" and insert it in the oven.
11. After 2 minutes of cooking, spray both sides of the bread strips with cooking spray.
12. Serve immediately with the topping of icing sugar.

Nutrition

Calories 41 | Fat 2.8g | Saturated Fat 1.5g | Cholesterol 32mg | Sodium 72mg | Carbs 3g | Fiber 0.1g | Sugar 1.5g | Protein 1.2g

57. Polenta Sticks

⏰ Prep Time 15 m | ⏰ Cooking Time 6 m | 4 Servings

Ingredients

- 1 tablespoon oil
- 2½ cups cooked polenta
- Salt, to taste
- ¼ cup Parmesan cheese

Directions

1. Place the polenta in a lightly greased baking pan.
2. With a plastic wrap, cover, and refrigerate for about 1 hour or until set.
3. Remove from the refrigerator and cut into desired sized slices.
4. Sprinkle with salt.
5. Press the "Power Button" of Air Fry Oven and turn the dial to select the "Air Fry" mode.
6. Press the Time button and again turn the dial to set the cooking time to 6 minutes.
7. Now push the Temp button and rotate the dial to set the temperature at 350 degrees F.
8. Press the "Start/Pause" button to start.
9. When the unit beeps to show that it is preheated, open the lid.
10. Arrange the pan over the "Wire Rack" and insert it in the oven.
11. Top with cheese and serve.

Nutrition

Calories 397 | Fat 5.6g | Saturated Fat 1.3g | Cholesterol 4mg | Sodium 127mg | Carbs 76.2g | Fiber 2.5g | Sugar 1g | Protein 9.1g

58. Crispy Eggplant Slices

⏰ Prep Time 15 m | ⏰ Cooking Time 8 m | 4 Servings

Ingredients

- 1 medium eggplant, shredded and cut into ½-inch round slices
- Salt, as required
- ½ cup all-purpose flour
- 2 eggs, beaten
- 1 cup Italian-style breadcrumbs
- ¼ cup olive oil

Directions

1. In a colander, add the eggplant slices and sprinkle with salt. Set aside for about 45 minutes.
2. With paper towels, pat dries the eggplant slices.
3. In a shallow dish, place the flour.
4. Crack the eggs in a second dish and beat well.
5. In a third dish, mix together the oil and breadcrumbs.
6. Coat each eggplant slice with flour, then dip into beaten eggs, and finally, coat with the breadcrumbs mixture.
7. Press the "Power Button" of Air Fry Oven and turn the dial to select the "Air Fry" mode.
8. Press the Time button and again turn the dial to set the cooking time to 8 minutes.
9. Now push the Temp button and rotate the dial to set the temperature at 390 degrees F.
10. Press the "Start/Pause" button to start.
11. When the unit beeps to show that it is preheated, open the lid.
12. Arrange the eggplant slices in "Air Fry Basket" and insert it in the oven.
13. Serve warm.

Nutrition

Calories 332 | Fat 16.6g | Saturated Fat 2.8g | Cholesterol 82 mg | Sodium 270mg | Carbs 38.3g | Fiber 5.7g | Sugar 5.3g | Protein 9.1g

59. Simple Cauliflower Poppers

⏰ Prep Time 10 m | ⏰ Cooking Time 8 m | 4 Servings

Ingredients

- ½ large head cauliflower, cut into bite-sized florets
- One tablespoon olive oil
- Salt and ground black pepper, as required

Directions

1. In a large bowl, add all the ingredients and toss to coat well.
2. Press the "Power Button" of Air Fry Oven and turn the dial to select the "Air Fry" mode.
3. Press the Time button and again turn the dial to set the cooking time to 8 minutes.
4. Now push the Temp button and rotate the dial to set the temperature at 390 degrees F.
5. Press the "Start/Pause" button to start.
6. When the unit beeps to show that it is preheated, open the lid.
7. Arrange the cauliflower florets in "Air Fry Basket" and insert it in the oven.
8. Toss the cauliflower florets once halfway through.
9. Serve warm.

Nutrition

Calories 138 | Fat 23.5g | Saturated Fat 0.5g | Cholesterol 0mg | Sodium 49mg | Carbs 1.8g | Fiber 0.8g | Sugar 0.8g | Protein 0.7g

60. Crispy Cauliflower Poppers

⏰ Prep Time 10 m | ⏰ Cooking Time 20 m | 4 Servings

Ingredients

- 1 egg white
- 1½ tablespoons ketchup
- 1 tablespoon hot sauce
- 1/3 cup panko breadcrumbs
- 2 cups cauliflower florets

Directions

1. In an open bowl, mix together the egg white, ketchup, and hot sauce.
2. In another bowl, place the breadcrumbs.
3. Dip the cauliflower florets in ketchup mixture and then coat with the breadcrumbs.
4. Press the "Power Button" of Air Fry Oven and turn the dial to select the "Air Fry" mode.
5. Press the Time button and again turn the dial to set the cooking time to 20 minutes.
6. Now push the Temp button and rotate the dial to set the temperature at 320 degrees F.
7. Press the "Start/Pause" button to start.
8. When the unit beeps to show that it is preheated, open the lid.
9. Arrange the cauliflower florets in "Air Fry Basket" and insert it in the oven.
10. Toss the cauliflower florets once halfway through.
11. Serve warm.

Nutrition

Calories 55 | Fat 0.7g | Saturated Fat 0.3g | Cholesterol 0mg | Sodium 181mg | Carbs 5.6g | Fiber 1.3g | Sugar 2.6g | Protein 2.3g

61. Broccoli Poppers

⏰ Prep Time 15 m | ⏱ Cooking Time 10 m | 4 Servings

Ingredients

- 2 tablespoons plain yogurt
- ½ teaspoon red chili powder
- ¼ teaspoon ground cumin
- ¼ teaspoon ground turmeric
- Salt, to taste
- 1 lb. broccoli, cut into small florets
- 2 tablespoons chickpea flour

Directions

1. In an open bowl, mix together the yogurt, and spices.
2. Add the broccoli and coat with marinade generously.
3. Refrigerate for about 20 minutes.
4. Press the "Power Button" of Air Fry Oven and turn the dial to select the "Air Fry" mode.
5. Press the Time button and again turn the dial to set the cooking time to 10 minutes.
6. Now push the Temp button and rotate the dial to set the temperature at 400 degrees F.
7. Press the "Start/Pause" button to start.
8. When the unit beeps to show that it is preheated, open the lid.
9. Arrange the broccoli florets in "Air Fry Basket" and insert it in the oven.
10. Toss the broccoli florets once halfway through.
11. Serve warm.

Nutrition

Calories 69 | Fat 0.9g | Saturated Fat 0.1g | Cholesterol 0mg | Sodium 87mg | Carbs 12.2 g | Fiber 4.2g | Sugar 3.2g | Protein 4.9g

62. Cheesy Broccoli Bites

⏰ Prep Time 15 m | ⏱ Cooking Time 12 m | 5 Servings

Ingredients

- 1 cup broccoli florets
- 1 egg, beaten
- ¾ cup cheddar cheese, grated
- 2 tablespoons Parmesan cheese, grated
- ¾ cup panko breadcrumbs
- Salt and freshly ground black pepper, as needed

Directions

1. In a food processor, add the broccoli and pulse until finely crumbled.
2. In a large bowl, mix together the broccoli and remaining ingredients.
3. Make small equal-sized balls from the mixture.
4. Press the "Power Button" of Air Fry Oven and turn the dial to select the "Air Fry" mode.
5. Press the Time button and again turn the dial to set the cooking time to 12 minutes.
6. Now push the Temp button and rotate the dial to set the temperature at 350 degrees F.
7. Press the "Start/Pause" button to start.
8. When the unit beeps to show that it is preheated, open the lid.
9. Arrange the broccoli balls in "Air Fry Basket" and insert them in the oven.
10. Serve warm.

Nutrition

Calories 153 | Fat 8.2 g | Fat 4.5g | Cholesterol 52mg | Sodium 172mg | Carbs 4g | Fiber 0.5g | Sugar 0.5g | Protein 7.1g

63. Mixed Veggie Bites

⏱ Prep Time 15 m | ⏱ Cooking Time 10 m | 5 Servings

Ingredients

- ¾ lb. fresh spinach, blanched, drained, and chopped
- ¼ of onion, chopped
- ½ of carrot, peeled and chopped
- 1 garlic clove, minced
- 1 American cheese slice, cut into tiny pieces
- 1 bread slice, toasted and processed into breadcrumbs
- ½ tablespoon cornflour
- ½ teaspoon red chili flakes
- Salt, as required

Directions

1. Place all ingredients in a bowl, except breadcrumbs, and mix until well combined.
2. Add the breadcrumbs and gently stir to combine.
3. Make 10 equal-sized balls from the mixture.
4. Press the "Power Button" of Air Fry Oven and turn the dial to select the "Air Fry" mode.
5. Press the Time button and again turn the dial to set the cooking time to 10 minutes.
6. Now push the Temp button and rotate the dial to set the temperature at 355 degrees F.
7. Press the "Start/Pause" button to start.
8. When the unit beeps to show that it is preheated, open the lid.
9. Arrange the veggie balls in "Air Fry Basket" and insert them in the oven.
10. Serve warm.

Nutrition

Calories 43 | Fat 1.4g | Saturated Fat 0.7g | Cholesterol 3mg | Sodium 155mg | Carbs 5.6g | Fiber 1.9g | Sugar 1.2g | Protein 3.1g

64. Risotto Bites

⏱ Prep Time 15 m | ⏱ Cooking Time 10 m | 4 Servings

Ingredients

- 1½ cups cooked risotto
- 3 tablespoons Parmesan cheese, grated
- ½ egg, beaten
- 1½ oz. mozzarella cheese, cubed
- 1/3 cup breadcrumbs

Directions

1. In a bowl, add the risotto, Parmesan, and egg and mix until well combined.
2. Make 20 equal-sized balls from the mixture.
3. Insert a mozzarella cube in the center of each ball.
4. With your fingers, smooth the risotto mixture to cover the ball.
5. In a shallow dish, place the breadcrumbs.
6. Coat the balls with the breadcrumbs evenly.
7. Press the "Power Button" of Air Fry Oven and turn the dial to select the "Air Fry" mode.
8. Press the Time button and again turn the dial to set the cooking time to 10 minutes.
9. Now push the Temp button and rotate the dial to set the temperature at 390 degrees F.
10. Press the "Start/Pause" button to start.
11. When the unit beeps to show that it is preheated, open the lid.
12. Arrange the balls in "Air Fry Basket" and insert them in the oven.
13. Serve warm.

Nutrition

Calories 340 | Fat 4.3g | Saturated Fat 2g | Cholesterol 29mg | Sodium 173mg | Carbs 62.4g | Fiber 1.3g | Sugar 0.7g | Protein 11.3g

65. Rice Flour Bites

⏰ Prep Time 15 m | ⏱ Cooking Time 12 m | 4 Servings

Ingredients

- 6 tablespoons milk
- ½ teaspoon vegetable oil
- ¾ cup of rice flour
- 1 oz. Parmesan cheese, shredded

Directions

1. In a bowl, add milk, flour, oil, and cheese and mix until a smooth dough forms.
2. Make small equal-sized balls from the dough.
3. Press the "Power Button" of Air Fry Oven and turn the dial to select the "Air Fry" mode.
4. Press the Time button and again turn the dial to set the cooking time to 12 minutes.
5. Now push the Temp button and rotate the dial to set the temperature at 300 degrees F.
6. Press the "Start/Pause" button to start.
7. When the unit beeps to show that it is preheated, open the lid.
8. Arrange the balls in "Air Fry Basket" and insert them in the oven.
9. Serve warm.

Nutrition

Calories 148 | Fat 3g | Saturated Fat 1.5g | Cholesterol 7mg | Sodium 77mg | Carbs 25.1g | Fiber 0.7g | Sugar 1.1g | Protein 4.8g

66. Lemon Parmesan and Peas Risotto

⏰ Prep Time 10 m | ⏱ Cooking Time 17 m | 6 Servings

Ingredients

- 2 tablespoons butter
- 1½ cup of rice
- 1 yellow onion, peeled and chopped
- 1 tablespoon extra-virgin olive oil
- 1 teaspoon lemon zest, grated
- 3½ cups chicken stock
- 2 tablespoons lemon juice
- 2 tablespoons parsley, diced
- 2 tablespoons Parmesan cheese, finely grated
- Salt and ground black pepper, to taste
- 1½ cup peas

Directions

1. Put the Instant Pot in the sauté mode, add 1 tablespoon of butter and oil, and heat them. Add the onion, mix, and cook for 5 minutes.
2. Add the rice, mix, and cook for another 3 minutes. Add 3 cups of broth and lemon juice, mix, cover, and cook for 5 minutes on rice.
3. Release the pressure, put the fryer in manual mode, add the peas and the rest of the broth, stir and cook for 2 minutes.
4. Add the cheese, parsley, remaining butter, lemon zest, salt, and pepper to taste and mix. Divide between plates and serve.

Nutrition

Calories 140 | Fat 1.5 g | Fiber 1 g | Carbohydrate 27 g | Proteins 5 g

67. Spinach and Goat Cheese Risotto

⏰ Prep Time 10 m | ⏱ Cooking Time 10 m | 6 Servings

Ingredients

- ¾ cup yellow onion, chopped
- 1½ cups Arborio rice
- 12 ounces' spinach, chopped
- 3½ cups hot vegetable stock
- ½ cup white wine
- 2 garlic cloves, peeled and minced
- 2 tablespoons extra virgin olive oil
- Salt and ground black pepper, to taste
- ⅓ cup pecans, toasted and chopped
- 4 ounces' goat cheese, soft and crumbled
- 2 tablespoons lemon juice

Directions

1. Put the Instant Pot in the sauté mode, add the oil and heat. Add garlic and onion, mix and cook for 5 minutes.
2. Add the rice, mix, and cook for 1 minute. Add wine, stir and cook until it is absorbed. Add 3 cups of stock, cover the Instant Pot, and cook the rice for 4 minutes.
3. Release the pressure, uncover the Instant Pot, add the spinach, stir and cook for 3 minutes in Manual mode. Add salt, pepper, the rest of the stock, lemon juice, and goat cheese and mix. Divide between plates, decorate with nuts and serve.

Nutrition

Calories 340 | Fat 23 g | Fiber 4.5 g | Carbohydrate 24 g | Proteins 18.9 g

68. Rice and Artichokes

⏰ Prep Time 10 m | ⏱ Cooking Time 20 m | 4 Servings

Ingredients

- 2 garlic cloves, peeled and crushed
- 1¼ cups chicken broth
- 1 tablespoon extra-virgin olive oil
- 5 ounces Arborio rice
- 1 tablespoon white wine
- 15 ounces canned artichoke hearts, chopped
- 16 ounces' cream cheese
- 1 tablespoon grated Parmesan cheese
- 1½ tablespoons fresh thyme, chopped
- Salt and ground black pepper, to taste
- 6 ounces' graham cracker crumbs
- 1¼ cups water

Directions

1. Put the Instant Pot in the sauté mode, add the oil, heat, add the rice, and cook for 2 minutes. Add the garlic, mix, and cook for 1 minute.
2. Transfer to a heat-resistant plate. Add the stock, crumbs, salt, pepper, and wine, mix and cover the plate with aluminum foil.
3. Place the dish in the basket to cook the Instant Pot, add water, cover, and cook for 8 minutes on rice. Release the pressure, remove the dish, uncover, add cream cheese, parmesan, artichoke hearts, and thyme.
4. Mix well and serve.

Nutrition

Calories 240 | Fat 7.2 g | Fiber 5.1 g | Carbohydrate 34 g | Proteins 6 g

69. Potatoes Au Gratin

⏱ Prep Time 10 m | ⏱ Cooking Time 17 m | 6 Servings

Ingredients

- ½ cup yellow onion, chopped
- 2 tablespoons butter
- 1 cup chicken stock
- 6 potatoes, peeled and sliced
- ½ cup sour cream
- Salt and ground black pepper, to taste
- 1 cup Monterey jack cheese, shredded
- For the topping:
- 3 tablespoons melted butter
- 1 cup breadcrumbs

Directions

1. Put the Instant Pot in Saute mode, add the butter and melt. Add the onion, mix, and cook for 5 minutes. Add the stock, salt, and pepper and put the steamer basket in the Instant Pot also.
2. Add the potatoes, cover the Instant Pot, and cook for 5 minutes in the Manual setting. In a bowl, mix 3 tablespoons of butter with breadcrumbs and mix well. Relieve the pressure of the Instant Pot, remove the steam basket, and transfer the potatoes to a pan.
3. Pour the cream and cheese into the instant pot and mix. Add the potatoes and mix gently.
4. Spread breadcrumbs, mix everywhere, place on a preheated grill, and cook for 7 minutes. Let cool for more minutes and serve.

Nutrition

Calories 340 | Fat 22 g | Fiber 2 g | Carbohydrate 32 g | Proteins 11 g

Beef, Lamb & Pork Recipes

70. Cheeseburger Egg Rolls

⏰ Prep Time 10 m | ⏱ Cooking Time 7 m | 6 Servings

Ingredients

- 6 egg roll wrappers
- 6 chopped dill pickle chips
- 1 tbsp. yellow mustard
- 3 tbsp. cream cheese
- 3 tbsp. shredded cheddar cheese
- ½ C. chopped onion
- ½ C. chopped bell pepper
- ¼ tsp. onion powder
- ¼ tsp. garlic powder
- 8 ounces of raw lean ground beef

Directions

1. In a skillet, add the spices, meat, onion, and bell pepper. Stir and mash the meat until it is fully cooked and the vegetables are soft.
2. Remove skillet from heat and add cream cheese, mustard, and cheddar cheese, stirring until melted.
3. Pour the meat mixture into a bowl and add the pickles.
4. Place egg wrappers and spoon 1/6 of the meat mixture into each. Dampen the edges of the egg roll with water. Fold the sides in half and seal with water.
5. Repeat with all the other egg rolls.
6. Place the rolls in a deep fryer, one batch at a time.
7. Pour into the Oven rack/basket. Place the air fryer Rack on the middle-shelf of the Smart Air Fryer Oven. Set temperature to 391°F, and set time to 7 minutes.

Nutrition

Calories 153 | Fat 4 g | Protein 12 g | Sugar 3 g

71. Air Fried Grilled Steak

⏰ Prep Time 5 m | ⏱ Cooking Time 45 m | 2 Servings

Ingredients

- Top sirloin steaks
- Tablespoons butter, melted
- 3 tablespoons olive oil
- Salt and pepper to taste

Directions

1. Preheat the Smart Air Fryer for 5 minutes.
2. Season the sirloin steaks with olive oil, salt, and pepper.
3. Place the beef in the air fryer oven basket.
4. Cook for 45 minutes at 350°F.
5. Once cooked, serve with butter.

Nutrition

Calories 1536 | Fat 123.7 g | Protein 103.4 g

72. Juicy Cheeseburgers

⏰ Prep Time 5 m | ⏲ Cooking Time 15 m | 4 Servings

Ingredients

- 1 pound 93% lean ground beef
- 1 teaspoon Worcestershire sauce
- 1 tablespoon burger seasoning
- Salt
- Pepper
- Cooking oil
- Slices cheese
- Buns

Directions

1. In a large bowl, combine the ground beef, Worcestershire, hamburger seasoning, and salt and pepper to taste until well combined. Spray the fryer basket with cooking oil. You will only need a quick spray because hamburgers produce oil while they cook. Form 4 patties with the mixture. Place the burgers in the deep fryer. Burgers should fit without having to be stacked, but stacking is fine if necessary.

2. Place on the oven rack/basket. Place the rack on the middle shelf of the Smart Air Fryer. Set the temperature to 375 ° F and set the time to 8 minutes. Cook for 8 minutes. Open the fryer and flip the patties—Cook for 3 to 4 more minutes. Check the inside of the patties to see if they have finished cooking. You can stick a knife or fork in the center to examine the color.

3. Fill each burger with a slice of cheese. Cook for one more minute or until cheese is melted. Serve on buns with any additional toppings of your choice.

Nutrition

Calories 566 | Fat 39 g | Protein 29 g | Fiber 1 g

73. Spicy Thai Beef Stir-Fry

⏰ Prep Time 15 m | ⏲ Cooking Time 9 m | 4 Servings

Ingredients

- 1 pound sirloin steaks, thinly sliced
- Tablespoons lime juice, divided
- ⅓ cup crunchy peanut butter
- ½ cup beef broth
- 1 tablespoon olive oil
- 1½ cups broccoli florets
- Cloves garlic, sliced
- 1 to 2 red chile peppers, sliced

Directions

1. In a medium bowl, combine the steak with 1 tablespoon of the lime juice. Set aside.

2. Combine the peanut butter and beef broth in a small bowl and mix well. Drain the beef and add the juice from the bowl into the peanut butter mixture.

3. In a 6-inch metal bowl, combine the olive oil, steak, and broccoli.

4. Pour into the Oven rack/basket. Place the air fryer Rack on the middle-shelf of the Smart Air Fryer Oven. Set temperature to 375°F, and set time to 4 minutes. Cook for 4 more minutes or until the steak is almost cooked and the broccoli is crisp and tender, shaking the basket once during cooking time.

5. Add the garlic, chile peppers, and the peanut butter mixture and stir.

6. Cook for 5 more minutes or until the sauce is bubbling and the broccoli is tender.

7. Serve over hot rice.

Nutrition

Calories 387 | Fat 22 g | Protein 42 g | Fiber 2 g

74. Beef Brisket Recipe from Texas

⏰ Prep Time 15 m | ⏱ Cooking Time 1 h 30 m | 8 Servings

Ingredients

- 1 ½ cup beef stock
- 1 bay leaf
- 1 tablespoon garlic powder
- 1 tablespoon onion powder
- Pounds beef brisket, trimmed
- 2 tablespoons chili powder
- 2 teaspoons dry mustard
- Tablespoons olive oil
- Salt and pepper to taste

Directions

1. Preheat the Air Fryer Oven for 5 minutes. Place all ingredients in a deep baking dish that will fit in the air fryer.

2. Bake for 1 hour and 30 minutes at 400°F.
3. Stir the beef every after 30 minutes to soak in the sauce.

Nutrition

Calories 306 | Fat 24.1 g | Protein 18.3 g

75. Copycat Taco Bell Crunch Wraps

⏰ Prep Time 10 m | ⏱ Cooking Time 2 m | 6 Servings

Ingredients

- Wheat tostadas
- C. sour cream
- 2 C. Mexican blend cheese
- 2 C. shredded lettuce
- 12 ounces low-sodium nacho cheese
- Roma tomatoes
- 12-inch wheat tortillas
- 1 1/3 C. water
- 2 packets low-sodium taco seasoning
- 2 pounds of lean ground beef

Directions

1. Ensure your air fryer is preheated to 400 degrees.
2. Make beef according to taco seasoning packets.
3. Place 2/3 C. prepared beef, 4 tbsp. cheese, 1 tostada, 1/3 C. sour cream, 1/3 C. lettuce, 1/6th of tomatoes, and 1/3 C. cheese on each tortilla.

4. Fold up tortillas edges and repeat with remaining ingredients.
   Lay the folded sides of tortillas down into the air fryer and spray with olive oil.
5. Set temperature to 400°F, and set time to 2 minutes. Cook 2 minutes until browned.

Nutrition

Calories 311 | Fat 9g | Protein 22g | Sugar 2g

76. Steak and Mushroom Gravy

⏲ Prep Time 15 m | ⏲ Cooking Time 15 m | 4 Servings

Ingredients

- Cubed steaks
- 2 large eggs
- 1/2 dozen mushrooms
- Tablespoons unsalted butter
- Tablespoons black pepper
- 2 tablespoons salt
- 1/2 teaspoon onion powder

- 1/2 teaspoon garlic powder
- 1/4 teaspoon cayenne powder
- 1 1/4 teaspoons paprika
- 1 1/2 cups whole milk
- 1/3 cup flour
- Tablespoons vegetable oil

Directions

1. Mix 1/2 flour and a pinch of black pepper in a shallow bowl or on a plate.
2. Beat 2 eggs in a bowl and mix with a pinch of salt and pepper.
3. In another shallow bowl, mix the other half of the flour with pepper to taste, garlic powder, paprika, cayenne, and onion powder.
4. Chop the mushrooms and reserve.
5. Squeeze the fillet into the first bowl of flour, then dip it into the egg and then press the fillet into the second bowl of flour until completely covered.
6. Place on the oven rack/basket. Place the rack on the middle shelf of the Smart Air Fryer. Set the temperature to 360 ° F and set the time to 15 minutes by turning it halfway.
7. While the steak is cooking, heat the butter over medium heat and add the mushrooms to the stir-fry.
8. Add 4 tablespoons of flour and pepper to the skillet and mix until there are no lumps of flour.
9. Mix in whole milk and simmer.

Nutrition

Calories 442 | Fat 27 g | Protein 32 g | Fiber 2.3 g

77. Air Fryer Beef Casserole

⏰ Prep Time 5 m | ⏰ Cooking Time 30 m | 4 Servings

Ingredients

- 1 green bell pepper, seeded and chopped
- 1 onion, chopped
- 1-pound ground beef
- Cloves of garlic, minced
- Tablespoons olive oil
- Cups eggs, beaten
- Salt and pepper to taste

Directions

1. Preheat the Smart Air Fryer oven for 5 minutes.
2. In a skillet that will fit in the deep fryer, combine the ground beef, onion, garlic, olive oil, and pepper. Season with salt and pepper to taste.
3. Add the beaten eggs and mix well.
4. Place the plate with the meat and egg mixture in the deep fryer.
5. Place on the oven rack/basket. Place the rack on the middle shelf of the Smart Air Fryer. Set the temperature to 325 ° F and set the time to 30 minutes. Bake for 30 minutes.

Nutrition

Calories 1520 | Fat 125.11 g | Protein 87.9 g

78. Meat Lovers' Pizza

⏰ Prep Time 10 m | ⏰ Cooking Time 12 m | 2 Servings

Ingredients

- 1 pre-prepared 7-inch pizza pie crust, defrosted if necessary
- 1/3 cup of marinara sauce.
- ounces of grilled steak, sliced into bite-sized pieces
- 2 ounces of salami, sliced fine
- 2 ounces of pepperoni, sliced fine
- ¼ cup of American cheese
- ¼ cup of shredded mozzarella cheese

Directions

1. Preheat the Smart Air Fryer Oven to 350 degrees. Lay the pizza dough flat on a sheet of parchment paper or tin foil, cut large enough to hold the entire pie crust, but small enough that it will leave the edges of the air frying basket uncovered to allow for air circulation.

2. Using a fork, stab the pizza dough several times across the surface – piercing the pie crust will allow air to circulate throughout the crust and ensure even cooking.

3. With a deep soup spoon, scoop the marinara sauce onto the pizza dough, and spread evenly in expanding circles over the surface of the pie-crust. Be sure to leave at least ½ inch of bare dough around the edges, to ensure that extra-crispy crunchy first bite of the crust!

4. Distribute the pieces of steak and the slices of salami and pepperoni evenly over the sauce-covered dough, then sprinkle the cheese in an even layer on top.

5. Set the air fryer timer to 12 minutes, and place the pizza with foil or paper on the fryer's basket surface. Again, be sure to leave the edges of the basket uncovered to allow for proper air circulation, and don't let your bare fingers touch the hot surface.

6. After 12 minutes, when the Smart Air Fryer Oven shuts off, the cheese should be perfectly melted and lightly crisped, and the pie crust should be golden brown. Using a spatula – or two, if necessary, remove the pizza from the air fryer basket and set on a serving plate.

7. Wait a few minutes until the pie is cool enough to handle, then cut into slices and serve.

Nutrition

Calories 342 | Fat 17 g | Protein 12 g | Fiber 4.3 g

79. Chimichurri Skirt Steak

⏰ Prep Time 10 m | ⏱ Cooking Time 8 m | 2 Servings

Ingredients

- x 8 oz. Skirt Steak
- 1 cup finely chopped parsley
- ¼ cup finely chopped mint
- 2 tbsp. fresh oregano (washed & finely chopped)
- Finely chopped cloves of garlic
- 1 tsp red pepper flakes (Crushed)
- 1 tbsp. ground cumin

- 1 tsp cayenne pepper
- 2 tsp smoked paprika
- 1 tsp salt
- ¼ tsp pepper
- ¾ cup oil
- Tbsp. red wine vinegar

Directions

1. Throw all the ingredients in a bowl (besides the steak) and mix well.
2. Put ¼ cup of the mixture in a plastic baggie with the steak and leave in the fridge overnight (2–24hrs).
3. Leave the bag out at room temperature for at least 30 min before popping into the air fryer. Preheat for a minute or two to 390° F before cooking until med–rare (8–10 min). Pour into the oven rack/basket. Place the air fryer Rack on the middle-shelf of the Smart Air Fryer Oven. Set temperature to 390°F, and set time to 10 minutes.
4. Put 2 tablespoons of the chimichurri mix on top of each steak before serving.

Nutrition

Calories 272 | Fat 3 g | Protein 32 g | Fiber 2.8 g

80. Country Fried Steak

⏰ Prep Time 5 m | ⏱ Cooking Time 12 m | 2 Servings

Ingredients

- 1 tsp. pepper
- C. almond milk
- 2 tbsp. almond flour
- Ounces ground sausage meat
- 1 tsp. pepper
- 1 tsp. salt

- 1 tsp. garlic powder
- 1 tsp. onion powder
- 1 C. panko breadcrumbs
- 1 C. almond flour
- Beaten eggs
- Ounces sirloin steak, pounded till thin

Directions

1. Season panko breadcrumbs with spices.
2. Dredge steak in flour, then egg, and then seasoned panko mixture.
3. Place into the air fryer basket.
4. Set temperature to 370°F, and set time to 12 minutes.
5. To make sausage gravy, cook sausage and drain off fat, but reserve 2 tablespoons.
6. Add flour to sausage and mix until incorporated. Gradually mix in milk over medium to high heat until it becomes thick.
7. Season mixture with pepper and cook 3 minutes longer.
8. Serve steak topped with gravy and enjoy.

Nutrition

Calories 395 | Fat 11 g | Protein 39 g | Sugar 5 g

81. Creamy Burger & Potato Bake

⏲ Prep Time 5 m | ⏲ Cooking Time 55 m | 3 Servings

Ingredients

- Salt to taste
- Freshly ground pepper, to taste
- 1/2 (10.75 ounces) can of condensed cream of mushroom soup
- 1/2-pound lean ground beef

- 1-1/2 cups peeled and thinly sliced potatoes
- 1/2 cup shredded cheddar cheese
- 1/4 cup chopped onion
- 1/4 cup and 2 tablespoons milk

Directions

1. Lightly grease baking pan of the air fryer with cooking spray. Add ground beef. For 10 minutes, cook on 360°F. Stir and crumble halfway through cooking time.
2. Meanwhile, in a bowl, whisk well pepper, salt, milk, onion, and mushroom soup. Mix well.
3. Drain fat off ground beef and transfer beef to a plate.

4. In the same air fryer baking pan, layer ½ of potatoes on the bottom, then ½ of soup mixture, and then ½ of beef. Repeat process.
5. Cover pan with foil.
6. Cook for 30 minutes. Remove the aluminum foil and cook for another 15 minutes or until potatoes are tender.
7. Serve and enjoy.

Nutrition

Calories 399 | Fat 26.9 g | Protein 22.1 g

82. Beefy 'n Cheesy Spanish Rice Casserole

⏲ Prep Time 10 m | ⏲ Cooking Time 50 m | 3 Servings

Ingredients

- Tablespoons chopped green bell pepper
- 1 tablespoon chopped fresh cilantro
- 1/2-pound lean ground beef
- 1/2 cup water
- 1/2 teaspoon salt
- 1/2 teaspoon brown sugar
- 1/2 pinch ground black pepper

- 1/3 cup uncooked long-grain rice
- 1/4 cup finely chopped onion
- 1/4 cup chile sauce
- 1/4 teaspoon ground cumin
- 1/4 teaspoon Worcestershire sauce
- 1/4 cup shredded Cheddar cheese
- 1/2 (14.5 ounces) can canned tomatoes

Directions

1. Lightly grease baking pan of the air fryer with cooking spray. Add ground beef.
2. For 10 minutes, cook on 360°F. Halfway through cooking time, stir and crumble beef. Discard excess fat.
3. Stir in pepper, Worcestershire sauce, cumin, brown sugar, salt, chile sauce, rice, water, tomatoes, green bell pepper,

and onion. Mix well. Cover pan with foil and cook for 25 minutes. Stirring occasionally.
4. Give it one last good stir, press down firmly, and sprinkle cheese on top.
5. Cook uncovered for 15 minutes at 390°F until tops are lightly browned.
6. Serve and enjoy with chopped cilantro.

Nutrition

Calories 346 | Fat: 19.1 g | Protein 18.5 g

83. Warming Winter Beef with Celery

⏰ Prep Time 5 m | ⏰ Cooking Time 12 m | 4 Servings

Ingredients

- 9 ounces tender beef, chopped
- 1/2 cup leeks, chopped
- 1/2 cup celery stalks, chopped
- Cloves garlic, smashed
- Tablespoons red cooking wine

- 3/4 cup cream of celery soup
- 2 sprigs rosemary, chopped
- 1/4 teaspoon smoked paprika
- 3/4 teaspoons salt
- Salt and 1/4 teaspoon black pepper to taste

Directions

1. Add the beef, leeks, celery, and garlic to the baking dish; cook for about 5 minutes at 390 degrees F.

2. Once the meat is starting to tender, pour in the wine and soup. Season with rosemary, smoked paprika, salt, and black pepper. Now, cook an additional 7 minutes.

Nutrition

Calories 312 | Fat 17 g | Protein 22 g | Fiber 32 g

84. Beef & Veggie Spring Rolls

⏰ Prep Time 5 m | ⏰ Cooking Time 12 m | 10 Servings

Ingredients

- 2-ounce Asian rice noodles
- 1 tablespoon sesame oil
- 7-ounce ground beef
- 1 small onion, chopped
- garlic cloves, crushed

- 1 cup of fresh mixed vegetables
- 1 teaspoon soy sauce
- 1 packet spring roll skins
- Tablespoons water
- Olive oil, as required

Directions

1. Soak the noodles in warm water till it becomes soft.
2. Drain and cut into small lengths. In a pan heat the oil and add the onion and garlic and sauté for about 4-5 minutes.
3. Add beef and cook for about 4-5 minutes.
4. Add vegetables and cook for about 5-7 minutes or till cooked through.
5. Stir in soy sauce and remove from the heat.
6. Immediately, stir in the noodles and keep aside till all the juices have been absorbed.
7. Preheat the Smart Air Fryer Oven to 350 degrees F.
8. Place the spring rolls skin onto a smooth surface.
9. Add a line of the filling diagonally across.
10. Fold the top point over the filling and then fold in both sides.
11. On the final point brush it with water before rolling to seal.
12. Brush the spring rolls with oil.
13. Arrange the rolls in batches in the air fryer and cook for about 8 minutes.
14. Repeat with remaining rolls. Now, place spring rolls onto a baking sheet.
15. Bake for about 6 minutes per side.

Nutrition

Calories 532 | Fat 8 g | Protein 31 g | Fiber 12.3 g

85. Asian Inspired Sichuan Lamb

⏰ Prep Time 5 m | ⏰ Cooking Time 10 m | 4 Servings

Ingredients

- 1 ½ tablespoons cumin seed (do not use ground cumin)
- 1 teaspoon Sichuan peppers or ½ teaspoon cayenne
- 2 tablespoons vegetable oil
- 1 tablespoon garlic, peeled and minced
- 1 tablespoon light soy sauce
- 2 red chili peppers, seeded and chopped (use gloves)
- ¼ teaspoon granulated sugar
- ½ teaspoon salt
- 1 pound lamb shoulder, cut in ½ to 1-inch pieces
- 2 green onions, chopped
- 1 handful fresh cilantro, chopped

Directions

1. Turn on the burner to medium-high on the stove and heat up a dry skillet. Pour in the cumin seed and Sichuan peppers or cayenne and toast until fragrant. Turn off the burner and set aside until they are cool. Grind them in a grinder or mortar and pestle.

2. In a large bowl that will contain the marinade and the lamb, combine the vegetable oil, garlic, soy sauce, chili peppers, granulated sugar, and salt. Pour in the cumin/pepper combination and mix well.

3. Using a fork, poke holes in the lamb all over the top and bottom. Place the lamb in the marinade, cover, and refrigerate. You can also use a closeable plastic bag.

4. Preheat the air fryer to 360 degrees for 5 minutes.

5. Spray the basket with cooking spray.

6. Remove the lamb pieces from the marinade with tongs or slotted spoon and place them in the basket of the air fryer in a single layer. You may need to do more than 1 batch.

7. Cook for 10 minutes, flipping over 1 halfway through. Make sure the lamb's internal temperature is 145 degrees F with a meat thermometer. Put on a serving platter and repeat with the rest of the lamb.

8. Sprinkle the chopped green onions and cilantro over top, stir and serve.

Nutrition

Calories 142 | Fat 7 g | Protein 17 g | Fiber 4 g

86. Garlic and Rosemary Lamb Cutlets

⏰ Prep Time 30 m | ⏱ Cooking Time 25 m | 2 Servings

Ingredients

- 2 lamb racks (with 3 cutlets per rack)
- 2 cloves garlic, peeled and thinly sliced into slivers
- 2 long sprigs of fresh rosemary, leaves removed
- 2 tablespoons wholegrain mustard
- 1 tablespoon honey
- 2 tablespoons mint sauce (I use mint jelly)

Directions

1. Trim fat from racks and cut slits with a sharp knife in the top of the lamb. Insert slices of the garlic and rosemary leaves in the slits and set the lamb aside.
2. Make the marinade by whisking the mustard, honey, and mint sauce together and brush over the lamb racks. Let the marinade in a cool area for 20 minutes.
3. Preheat the air fryer to 360 degrees for about 5 minutes.
4. Spray the basket using cooking spray and place the lamb rack or racks into the basket, propping them up however you can get them in to fit.
5. Cook 10 minutes, open and turn the racks and cook 10 more minutes.
6. Place on a platter and cover with foil to let sit 10 minutes before slicing and serving.

Nutrition

Calories 309 | Fat 2 g | Protein 33 g | Fiber 16 g

87. Garlic Sauced Lamb Chops

⏰ Prep Time 15 m | ⏱ Cooking Time 25 m | 4 Servings

Ingredients

- 1 garlic bulb
- 1 teaspoon + 3 tablespoons olive oil
- 1 tablespoon fresh oregano, chopped fine
- ¼ teaspoon ground pepper
- ½ teaspoon sea salt
- 8 lamb chops

Directions

1. Preheat the air fryer to 400 degrees F 5 minutes and while it is preheating take the excess paper from the garlic bulb.
2. Coat the garlic bulb with the 1 teaspoon of olive oil and drop it in the basket that has been treated with cooking spray. Roast for 12 minutes.
3. Combine the 3 tablespoons of olive oil, oregano, salt, and pepper and lightly coat the lamb chops on both with the resulting oil. Let them sit at room temperature for 5 minutes.
4. Remove the garlic bulb from the basket and if it is cool, preheat again to 400 degrees for 3 minutes.
5. Spray the air fryer basket with cooking oil and place 4 chops in cooking at 400 degrees F for 5 minutes. Place them on a platter and cover to keep them warm while you do the other chops.
6. Squeeze each garlic clove between the thumb and index finger into a small bowl.
7. Taste and add salt and pepper and mix. Serve along with the chops like serving ketchup.

Nutrition

Calories 194 | Fat 11 g | Protein 29 g | Fiber 13 g

88. Herb Encrusted Lamb Chops

⏱ Prep Time 5 m | ⏱ Cooking Time 15 m | 2 Servings

Ingredients

- 1 teaspoon oregano
- 1 teaspoon coriander
- 1 teaspoon thyme
- 1 teaspoon rosemary
- ½ teaspoon salt
- ¼ teaspoon pepper
- 2 tablespoons lemon juice
- 2 tablespoons olive oil
- 1 pound lamb chops

Directions

1. In a closeable bag, combine the oregano, coriander, thyme, rosemary, salt, pepper, lemon juice, and olive oil and shake well so it mixes.
2. Place the chops in the bag and squish around so the mixture is on them. Refrigerate 1 hour.
3. Preheat the air fryer to 390 degrees F for 5 minutes.
4. Place the chops in the basket that has been sprayed with cooking spray.
5. Cook for 3 minutes and pause. Flip the chops to the other side and cook for another 4 minutes for medium rare. If you want them more well done, cook 4 minutes, pause, turn and cook 5 more minutes.

Nutrition

Calories 321 | Fat 34g | Protein 18 g | Fiber 15 g

89. Herbed Rack of Lamb

⏱ Prep Time 15 m | ⏱ Cooking Time 35 m | 2 Servings

Ingredients

- 1 tablespoon olive oil
- 1 clove garlic, peeled and minced
- 1 ½ teaspoons fresh ground pepper
- 1 tablespoon fresh rosemary, chopped
- 1 tablespoon fresh thyme, chopped
- ¾ cup breadcrumbs
- 1 egg
- 1 to 2 pounds rack of lamb

Directions

1. Place the olive oil in a small dish and add the garlic. Mix well.
2. Brush the garlic on the rack of lamb and season with pepper.
3. In one bowl combine the rosemary, thyme, and breadcrumbs and break the egg and whisk in another bowl.
4. Preheat air fryer 350 degrees F for 5 minutes. Spray with cooking spray.
5. Dip the rack in the egg and then place in the breadcrumb mixture and coat the rack.
6. Place rack in the air fryer basket and cook 20 minutes.
7. Raise the temperature to 400 degrees F and set for 5 more minutes.
8. Tear a piece of aluminum foil that will fit to wrap the rack. Take it out of the basket with tongs and put it in the middle of the foil. Carefully wrap and let sit about 10 minutes. Unwrap and serve.

Nutrition

Calories 282 | Fat 23 g | Protein 26 g | Fiber 23 g

90. Lamb Roast with Root Vegetables

⏱ Prep Time 35 m | ⏱ Cooking Time 1 h 15 m | 6 Servings

Ingredients

- 4 cloves garlic, peeled and sliced thin, divided
- 2 springs fresh rosemary, leaves pulled off, divided
- 3 pounds leg of lamb
- salt and pepper to taste, divided
- 2 medium-sized sweet potatoes, peeled and cut into wedges

- 2 tablespoon oil, divided
- 2 cups baby carrots
- 1 teaspoon butter
- 4 large red potatoes, cubed

Directions

1. Slice the garlic and take the leaves of the rosemary.
2. Cut about 5 to 6 slits in the top of the lamb and insert slices of garlic and some rosemary in each. Salt and pepper the roast to your taste and set aside to cook after the vegetables are done.
3. Coat the sweet potatoes in 1 tablespoon of olive oil and season with salt and pepper.
4. Spray the basket of the air fryer with cooking spray and put it in the wedges. You may have to do two batches. Set for 400 degrees F and air fry 8 minutes, shake and cook another 8 minutes or so. Dump into a bowl and cover with foil.
5. Place the carrots in some foil to cover and put the butter on top of them. Enclose them in the foil and place them in the air fryer. Set for 400 degrees for 20 minutes. Remove from the air fryer.
6. Coat the basket with cooking spray. Mix the red potatoes with the other tablespoon of oil and salt and pepper to taste. Place in the air fryer oven and cook at 400 degrees F for 20 minutes, shaking after 10 minutes have elapsed.
7. Use a foil tray or baking dish that fits into the air fryer and coat with cooking spray. Place the leftover garlic and rosemary in the bottom and place the lamb on top.
8. Set for 380 degrees F and cook 1 hour, checking after 30 minutes and 45 minutes to make sure it isn't getting too done. Increase the air fryer oven heat to 400 degrees F and cook for 10 to 15 minutes.
9. Remove the roast from the air fryer and set on a platter. Cover with foil and rest 10 minutes while you dump all the vegetables back in the basket and cooking at 350 degrees F for 8 to 10 minutes or until heated through.
10. Serve all together.

Nutrition

Calories 398 | Fat 5 g | Protein 18 g | Fiber 30.3 g

91. Lemon and Cumin Coated Rack of Lamb

Prep Time 15 m | Cooking Time 200 m | 4 Servings

Ingredients

- 1 ½ to 1 ¾ pound Frenched rack of lamb
- Salt and pepper to taste
- ½ cup breadcrumbs
- 1 teaspoon cumin seed
- 1 teaspoon ground cumin
- ½ teaspoon salt
- 1 teaspoon garlic, peeled and grated
- Lemon zest (1/4 of a lemon)
- 1 teaspoon vegetable or olive oil
- 1 egg, beaten

Directions

1. Season the lamb rack with pepper and salt to taste and set it aside.
2. In a large bowl, combine the breadcrumbs, cumin seed, ground cumin, salt, garlic, lemon zest, and oil and set aside.
3. In another bowl, beat the egg.
4. Preheat to air fryer to 250 degrees F for 5 minutes
5. Dip the rack in the egg to coat and then into the breadcrumb mixture. Make sure it is well coated.
6. Spray the basket of the air fryer using cooking spray and put the rack in. You may have to bend it a little to get it to fit.
7. Set for 250 degrees and cook 25 minutes.
8. Increase temperature to 400 degrees F and cook another 5 minutes. Check internal temperature to make sure it is 145 degrees for medium-rare or more.
9. Remove rack when done and cover with foil for 10 minutes before separating ribs into individual servings.

Nutrition

Calories 276 | Fat 24 g | Protein 33 g | Fiber 12.3 g

92. Macadamia Rack of Lamb

Prep Time 20 m | Cooking Time 32 m | 4 Servings

Ingredients

- 1 tablespoon olive oil
- 1 clove garlic, peeled and minced
- 1 ½ to 1 ¾ pound rack of lamb
- Salt and pepper to taste
- ¾ cup unsalted macadamia nuts
- 1 tablespoon fresh rosemary, chopped
- 1 tablespoon breadcrumbs
- 1 egg, beaten

Directions

1. Mix together the olive oil and garlic and brush it all over the rack of lamb. Season with salt and pepper.
2. Preheat the air fryer 250 degrees F for 8 minutes.
3. Chop the macadamia nuts as fine as possible and put them in a bowl.
4. Mix in the rosemary and breadcrumbs and set it aside.
5. Beat the egg in another bowl.
6. Dip the rack in the egg mixture to coat completely.
7. Place the rack in the breadcrumb mixture and coat well.
8. Spray the basket of the air fryer using cooking spray and place the rack inside.
9. Cook at 250 degrees for 25 minutes and then increase to 400 and cook another 5 to 10 minutes or until done.
10. Cover with foil paper for 10 minutes, uncover and separate into chops and serve.

Nutrition

Calories 321 | Fat 9 g | Protein 12 g | Fiber 8.3 g

93. Perfect Lamb Burgers

⏰ Prep Time 10 m | ⏰ Cooking Time 20 m | 4 Servings

Ingredients

For the Moroccan spice mix:

- 1 teaspoon ground ginger
- 1 teaspoon ground cumin
- 1 teaspoon sea salt
- ¾ teaspoon ground black pepper
- ½ teaspoon ground coriander
- ½ teaspoon ground allspice
- ½ teaspoon ground cloves
- ½ teaspoon ground cinnamon
- ½ teaspoon cayenne

For burgers and dip:

- 1 ½ pound ground lamb
- 1 teaspoon Harissa paste
- 2 tablespoons Moroccan spice mix, divided
- 2 teaspoons garlic, peeled and minced
- ¼ teaspoon fresh chopped oregano
- 3 tablespoons plain Greek yogurt
- 1 small lemon, juiced

Directions

Moroccan Spice Mix:

1. Whisk the ginger, cumin, salt, pepper, coriander, allspice, cloves, cinnamon, and cayenne in a small bowl and set aside.

Burgers and dip:

1. Place the lamb in a large bowl and add the Harissa sauce, 1 tablespoon of the homemade Moroccan spice mix, and the garlic. Mix in everything with the hands and form 4 patties.
2. Preheat the air fryer to 360 degrees for 5 minutes while making the patties.

3. Spray the basket of the air fryer using cooking spray and place two of the burgers in.
4. Cook a total of 12 minutes, flipping after 6 minutes.
5. Repeat with the other two burgers.
6. While burgers cook, make the dip by chopping the fresh oregano and placing it in a bowl with the yogurt, 1 teaspoon of the Moroccan spice mix, and the juice of the lemon. Whisk this with a fork and divide it into small containers to serve with the burgers when they are done.

Nutrition

Calories 534 | Fat 8 g | Protein 21 g | Fiber 8.7 g

94. Simple Yet Tasty Lamb Chops

⏱ Prep Time 15 m | ⏱ Cooking Time 30 m | 4 Servings

Ingredients

- 1 clove of garlic separated from the head of garlic (maybe 2)
- 1 ½ tablespoons olive oil
- 4 lamb chops
- ½ tablespoon fresh oregano, chopped
- Salt and pepper to taste

Directions

1. Preheat the air fryer oven to 400 degrees F for 6 minutes.
2. Take a little of the olive oil and coat the garlic clove(s). Place in the basket of the air fryer and roast 12 minutes.
3. While the garlic is cooking, mix the oregano, salt, and pepper in a small bowl. Add all the remaining olive oil and mix well.
4. Spread a thin coating of the oregano mixture on both sides of the lamb chops and reserve the rest.
5. Remove the clove(s) of garlic from the basket of the air fryer with rubber-tipped tongs. Be careful because the cloves will be very soft and you don't want them to break open quite yet.
6. Spray the basket of the air fryer using cooking spray and place the lamb chops in, 2 at a time in 2 batches. Cook 5 minutes, turn and cook another 4 minutes.
7. When chops are done, squeeze the garlic out of the papery shell into the rest of the oregano mixture and mix it in. Serve this on the side like ketchup.

Nutrition

Calories 542 | Fat 4 g | Protein 23 g | Fiber 6 g

95. Tandoori Lamb

⏱ Prep Time 10 m | ⏱ Cooking Time 20 m | 4 Servings

Ingredients

- ½ onion, peeled and quartered
- 5 cloves garlic, peeled
- 4 slices fresh ginger, peeled
- 1 teaspoon ground fennel
- 1 teaspoon Garam Masala
- 1 teaspoon ground cinnamon
- ½ teaspoon ground cardamom
- ½ teaspoon cayenne
- 1 teaspoon salt
- 1 pound boneless lamb sirloin steaks

Directions

1. Place the onion, garlic, ginger, fennel, Garam Masala, cinnamon, cardamom, cayenne, and salt in a blender and pulse 4 to 6 times until ground.
2. Place the lamb steaks in a large bowl and slash the meat so the spices will permeate into it.
3. Pour the spice mix over top and rub it on both sides. Let sit room temperature 30 minutes or cover and refrigerate overnight.
4. Preheat the air fryer to 350 degrees F for 10 minutes.
5. Spray the basket using cooking spray and place lamb steaks in without letting them overlap much. You may have to do this in batches.
6. Cook 7 minutes, turn and cook another 8 minutes.
7. Test with the meat thermometer to make sure they are done. The medium-well will be 150 degrees F.

Nutrition

Calories 232 | Fat 20 g | Protein 42 g | Fiber 5 g

96. Barbecue Flavored Pork Ribs

⏱ Prep Time 5 m | ⏱ Cooking Time 15 m | 6 Servings

Ingredients

- ¼ cup honey, divided
- ¾ cup BBQ sauce
- 2 tablespoons tomato ketchup
- 1 tablespoon Worcestershire sauce
- 1 tablespoon soy sauce
- ½ teaspoon garlic powder
- Freshly ground white pepper, to taste
- 1¾ pound pork ribs

Directions

1. In a large bowl, mix together 3 tablespoons of honey and remaining ingredients except for the pork ribs.
2. Refrigerate to marinate for about 20 minutes.
3. Preheat the Air fryer oven to 355 degrees F.
4. Place the ribs in an Air fryer rack/basket.
5. Cook for about 13 minutes.
6. Remove the ribs from the Air fryer oven and coat with remaining honey.
7. Serve hot.

Nutrition

Calories 376 | Fat 20 g | Protein 32 g | Fiber 12 g

97. Rustic Pork Ribs

⏱ Prep Time 5 m | ⏱ Cooking Time 15 m | 4 Servings

Ingredients

- 1 rack of pork ribs
- 3 tablespoons dry red wine
- 1 tablespoon soy sauce
- 1/2 teaspoon dried thyme
- 1/2 teaspoon onion powder
- 1/2 teaspoon garlic powder
- 1/2 teaspoon ground black pepper
- 1 teaspoon smoked salt
- 1 tablespoon cornstarch
- 1/2 teaspoon olive oil

Directions

1. Begin by preheating your Air fryer oven to 390 degrees F. Place all ingredients in a mixing bowl and let them marinate at least 1 hour.

Air Frying:

2. Cook the marinated ribs approximately 25 minutes at 390 degrees F.
3. Serve hot.

Nutrition

Calories 326 | Fat 14 g | Protein 23 g | Fiber 13 g

98. Italian Parmesan Breaded Pork Chops

⏲ Prep Time 5 m | ⏲ Cooking Time 25 m | 5 Servings

Ingredients

- 5 (3½- to 5-ounce) pork chops (bone-in or boneless)
- 1 teaspoon Italian seasoning
- Seasoning salt
- Pepper
- ¼ cup all-purpose flour
- 2 tablespoons Italian bread crumbs
- 3 tablespoons finely grated Parmesan cheese
- Cooking oil

Directions

1. Season the pork chops with the Italian seasoning and seasoning salt and pepper to taste.
2. Sprinkle the flour on each side of the pork chops, then coat both sides with the bread crumbs and Parmesan cheese.
3. Place the pork chops in the air fryer oven. Stacking them is okay. Spray the pork chops with cooking oil. Set temperature to 360°F. Cook for 6 minutes.
4. Open the air fryer oven and flip the pork chops. Cook for an additional 6 minutes.
5. Cool before serving. Instead of seasoning salt, you can use either chicken or pork rub for additional flavor. You can find these rubs in the spice aisle of the grocery store.

Nutrition

Calories 334 | Fat 7 g | Protein 34 g | Fiber 0 g

99. Crispy Breaded Pork Chops

⏲ Prep Time 10 m | ⏲ Cooking Time 15 m | 8 Servings

Ingredients

- 1/8 tsp. pepper
- ¼ tsp. chili powder
- ½ tsp. onion powder
- ½ tsp. garlic powder
- 1 ¼ tsp. sweet paprika
- tbsp. grated parmesan cheese
- 1/3 C. crushed cornflake crumbs
- ½ C. panko breadcrumbs
- 1 beaten egg
- 6 center-cut boneless pork chops

Directions

1. Ensure that your air fryer is preheated to 400 degrees. Spray the basket with olive oil.
2. With ½ teaspoon salt and pepper, season both sides of pork chops.
3. Combine ¾ teaspoon salt with pepper, chili powder, onion powder, garlic powder, paprika, cornflake crumbs, panko breadcrumbs, and parmesan cheese.
4. Beat egg in another bowl.
5. Dip the pork chops into the egg and then crumb mixture.
6. Add pork chops to air fryer and spritz with olive oil.

Air Frying:

1. Set temperature to 400°F, and set time to 12 minutes. Cook 12 minutes, making sure to flip over halfway through the cooking process.
2. Only add 3 chops in at a time and repeat the process with remaining pork chops.

Nutrition

Calories 378 | Fat 13 g | Protein 33 g | Sugar 1 g

100. Caramelized Pork Shoulder

⏰ Prep Time 10 m | ⏰ Cooking Time 20 m | 8 Servings

Ingredients

- 1/3 cup soy sauce

- tablespoons sugar

- 1 tablespoon honey

- 2 pounds pork shoulder, cut into 1½-inch thick slices

Directions

1. In a bowl, mix all the ingredients except pork.
2. Add pork and coat with marinade generously.
3. Cover and refrigerate o marinate for about 2-8 hours.
4. Preheat the Air fryer oven to 335 degrees F.
5. Place the pork in an Air fryer rack/basket.
6. Cook for about 10 minutes.
7. Now, set the Air fryer oven to 390 degrees F. Cook for about 10 minutes.

Nutrition

Calories 268 | Fat 10 g | Protein 23 g | Sugar 5 g

101. Roasted Pork Tenderloin

⏰ Prep Time 5 m | ⏰ Cooking Time 1 h | 4 Servings

Ingredients

- 1 (3-pound) pork tenderloin

- tablespoons extra-virgin olive oil

- 2 garlic cloves, minced

- 1 teaspoon dried basil

- 1 teaspoon dried oregano

- 1 teaspoon dried thyme

- Salt

- Pepper

Directions

1. Dip the pork fillet in olive oil.
2. Grate the garlic, basil, oregano, thyme, and salt and pepper to taste throughout the steak.
3. Place the steak in the oven of the deep fryer. Cook for 45 minutes.
4. Use a meat thermometer to check for politeness
5. Open the Air Fryer and flip the pork fillet. Cook for 15 more minutes.
6. Take the cooked pork out of the deep fryer and let it rest for 10 minutes before slicing it.

Nutrition

Calories 283 | Fat 10 g | Protein 48 g

102. Bacon-Wrapped Pork Tenderloin

⏰ Prep Time 5 m | ⏰ Cooking Time 15 m | 4 Servings

Ingredients

Pork:

- 1-2 tbsp. Dijon mustard
- 3-4 strips of bacon
- 1 pork tenderloin

Apple Gravy:

- ½ - 1 tsp. Dijon mustard

- 1 tbsp. almond flour
- tbsp. ghee
- 1 chopped onion
- 2-3 Granny Smith apples
- 1 C. vegetable broth

Directions

1. Spread Dijon mustard all over the tenderloin and wrap the meat with strips of bacon.
2. Place into the Air fryer oven, set the temperature to 360°F, and set time to 15 minutes, and cook 10-15 minutes at 360 degrees.
3. To make sauce, heat ghee in a pan and add shallots. Cook 1-2 minutes.
4. Then add apples, cooking 3-5 minutes until softened.

5. Add flour and ghee to make a roux. Add broth and mustard, stirring well to combine.
6. When the sauce starts to bubble, add 1 cup of sautéed apples, cooking till sauce thickens.
7. Once the pork tenderloin is cooked, let it sit 5-10 minutes to rest before slicing.
8. Serve topped with apple gravy.

Nutrition

Calories 552 | Fat 25 g | Protein 29 g | Sugar 6 g

103. Dijon Garlic Pork Tenderloin

⏰ Prep Time 5 m | ⏰ Cooking Time 10 m | 6 Servings

Ingredients

- 1 C. breadcrumbs
- Pinch of cayenne pepper
- Crushed garlic cloves
- 2 tbsp. ground ginger
- 2 tbsp. Dijon mustard

- 2 tbsp. raw honey
- tbsp. water
- 2 tsp. salt
- 1 pound pork tenderloin, sliced into 1-inch rounds

Directions

1. With pepper and salt, season all sides of the tenderloin.
2. Combine cayenne pepper, garlic, ginger, mustard, honey, and water until smooth.
3. Dip pork rounds into the honey mixture and then into breadcrumbs, ensuring they all get coated well.

4. Place coated pork rounds into your Air fryer oven.
5. Set temperature to 400°F, and set time to 10 minutes. Cook 10 minutes at 400 degrees. Flip and then cook an additional 5 minutes until golden in color.

Nutrition

Calories 423 | Fat 18 g | Protein 31 g | Sugar 3 g

104. Pork Neck with Salad

⏰ Prep Time 10 m | ⏱ Cooking Time 12 m | 2 Servings

Ingredients

For Pork:

- 1 tablespoon soy sauce
- 1 tablespoon fish sauce
- ½ tablespoon oyster sauce
- ½ pound pork neck

For Salad:

- 1 ripe tomato, sliced tickly
- 8-10 Thai shallots, sliced
- 1 scallion, chopped
- 1 bunch fresh basil leaves
- 1 bunch fresh cilantro leaves

For Dressing:

- Tablespoons fish sauce
- 2 tablespoons olive oil
- 1 teaspoon apple cider vinegar
- 1 tablespoon palm sugar
- 2 bird's eye chili
- 1 tablespoon garlic, minced

Directions

For the pork:

1. In a bowl, mix all the ingredients except the pork.
2. Add the pork neck and marinade layer evenly. Refrigerate for about 2-3 hours.
3. Preheat the deep fryer oven to 340 degrees F.
4. Air fry. Place the pork neck in a grill pan. Cook for about 12 minutes.

5. Meanwhile, in a large bowl, combine all of the salad ingredients.
6. In a bowl, add all the dressing ingredients and beat until well combined.
7. Remove the pork neck from the fryer and cut it into the desired slices.
8. Place the pork slices on top of the salad.

Nutrition

Calories 296 | Fat: 20 g | Protein 24 g | Sugar 8 g

105. Chinese Braised Pork Belly

⏰ Prep Time 5 m | ⏱ Cooking Time 20 m | 8 Servings

Ingredients

- 1 lb. pork belly, sliced
- 1 tbsp. oyster sauce
- 1 tbsp. sugar
- Red fermented bean curds
- 1 tbsp. red fermented bean curd paste
- 1 tbsp. cooking wine
- 1/2 tbsp. soy sauce
- 1 tsp sesame oil
- 1 cup all-purpose flour

Directions

1. Preheat the Air fryer oven to 390 degrees.
2. In a small bowl, mix up the ingredients together and rub the pork thoroughly with this mixture
3. Set aside to marinate for at least 30 minutes or preferably overnight for the flavors to permeate the meat

4. Coat each marinated pork belly slice in flour and place in the Air fryer oven tray
5. Cook for 20 minutes until crispy and tender.

Nutrition

Calories 409 | Fat 14 g | Protein 19 g | Sugar 9 g

106. Air Fryer Sweet and Sour Pork

⏰ Prep Time 10 m | ⏰ Cooking Time 12 m | 6 Servings

Ingredients

- Tbsp. olive oil
- 1/16 tsp. Chinese five-spice
- ¼ tsp. pepper
- ½ tsp. sea salt
- 1 tsp. pure sesame oil
- 2 eggs
- 1 C. almond flour
- 2 pounds pork, sliced into chunks

Sweet and Sour sauce:

- ¼ tsp. sea salt
- ½ tsp. garlic powder
- 1 tbsp. low-sodium soy sauce
- ½ C. rice vinegar
- tbsp. tomato paste
- 1/8 tsp. water
- ½ C. sweetener of choice

Directions

1. To make the dipping sauce, whisk all sauce ingredients together over medium heat, stirring 5 minutes. Simmer uncovered 5 minutes till thickened.
2. Meanwhile, combine almond flour, five-spice, pepper, and salt.
3. In another bowl, mix eggs with sesame oil.
4. Dredge pork in flour mixture and then in the egg mixture. Shake any excess off before adding to the air fryer rack/basket.
5. Set temperature to 340°F, and set time to 12 minutes.
6. Serve with sweet and sour dipping sauce!

Nutrition

Calories 371 | Fat 17 g | Protein 27 g | Sugar 1 g

107. Juicy Pork Ribs Ole

⏰ Prep Time 10 m | ⏰ Cooking Time 25 m | 4 Servings

Ingredients

- 1 rack of pork ribs
- 1/2 cup low-fat milk
- 1 tablespoon envelope taco seasoning mix
- 1 can tomato sauce
- 1/2 teaspoon ground black pepper
- 1 teaspoon seasoned salt
- 1 tablespoon cornstarch
- 1 teaspoon canola oil

Directions

1. Place all ingredients in a mixing dish; let them marinate for 1 hour.
2. Cook the marinated ribs approximately 25 minutes at 390 degrees F
3. Work with batches. Enjoy.

Nutrition

Calories 218 | Fat 8 g | Protein 11 g | Sugar 1 g

108. Teriyaki Pork Rolls

⏱ Prep Time 10 m | ⏱ Cooking Time 8 m | 6 Servings

Ingredients

- 1 tsp. almond flour
- tbsp. low-sodium soy sauce
- tbsp. mirin
- tbsp. brown sugar

- Thumb-sized amount of ginger, chopped
- Pork belly slices
- Enoki mushrooms

Directions

1. Mix brown sugar, mirin, soy sauce, almond flour, and ginger until brown sugar dissolves.
2. Take pork belly slices and wrap around a bundle of mushrooms. Brush each roll with teriyaki sauce. Chill half an hour.
3. Preheat your Air fryer oven to 350 degrees and add marinated pork rolls.
4. Set temperature to 350°F, and set time to 8 minutes.

Nutrition

Calories 412 | Fat 9 g | Protein 19 g | Sugar 4 g

Vegetarian Recipes

109. Air Fryer Buffalo Cauliflower

⏰ Prep Time 5 m | ⏰ Cooking Time 13 m | 6 Servings

Ingredients

- 2 medium head Cauliflowers which should be carefully chopped to florets that can be eaten in one scoop
- 4-6 tablespoons of red hot spice/sauce.
- ½ teaspoon of salt
- 2 tablespoon of arrowroot starch. You can also use cornstarch
- 3 teaspoons of maple syrup
- 4 spoons of your favorite avocado oil
- 4 tablespoons of nutritional yeast

Directions

1. First of all, make sure to cook with your Air Fryer at 360F.
2. Then add all your ingredients to a large bowl except the cauliflower.
3. Whisk the ingredients in the bowl until it is thorough.
4. Add the cauliflower and toss it to coat evenly.
5. Proceed to add half of your cauliflower to your new Air Fryer.
6. Cook for about 13 minutes and you can shake halfway through the cooking process.
7. If you have leftovers, then you can reheat in your Air Fryer for about 2 minutes.

Nutrition

Calories 118 | Fat 5 g | Protein 31 g | Sugar 5 g

110. Air Fryer Kale Chips

⏰ Prep Time 5 m | ⏰ Cooking Time 5 m | 2 Servings

Ingredients

- 1½ bunch of kale
- 1½ tbsp. oil
- Salt (to taste, preferably a pinch)
- Seasonings (as flavor): ranch or any of your choice

Directions

1. Wash kale under running water and dry.
2. Cut out the leaves and then, into small pieces into a bowl.
3. Pour oil into them and rub it vigorously into the leaves such that every piece is coated with oil.
4. Add salt, shaking the bowl sideways to make sure they are coated well.
5. Arrange kale into the air fryer basket while preventing overlapping and curling of leaves. Don't forget to cook them in batches if they cannot all fit into the basket at once.
6. Preheat the air fryer to 375°F.
7. Set the timer to 3-5 minutes and cook until they are crispy. So that they cook evenly, ensure you shake the basket at least once during cooking.
8. Serve warm while sprinkling the seasoning minimally as flavor to your kale chips.

Nutrition

Calories 345 | Fat 9 g | Protein 27 g | Sugar 7 g

111. Air Fried Mozzarella Stalks

⏱ Prep Time 5 m | ⏱ Cooking Time 10 m | 6 Servings

Ingredients

- 15 mozzarella sticks: cut from a block of cheese
- ½ cup general-purpose flour
- 2 Eggs
- 1½ cups breadcrumbs
- Spices: onion powder, garlic powder, smoked paprika (1 tsp. each) and salt (to taste).
- Sauce: any of your choice but for this book, we'll be using marinara

Directions

1. Make your mozzarella sticks by cutting them straight from cheese blocks (you may have them pre-cut though).
2. Arrange cheese sticks on a plate (parchment-lined for ease) and freeze in a freezer for about 40 minutes to prevent melting when placed into the air fryer.
3. You may seize your flour to remove air bubbles and place inside a covered bowl.
4. Break eggs and whisk well in a bowl.
5. Pour and mix spices and breadcrumb into a bowl.
6. Coat the mozzarella sticks evenly by placing them into the covered bowl or container, cover tightly, and shake. Open the bowl, take out the sticks one at a time, place into the whisked egg, and then into the mixture of the spices and crumbs.
7. Place the coated sticks back on the plate and freeze for about 30 minutes more this time around.
8. Get your air fryer out and clean it (you can do that before the whole cooking process though).
9. Grease the air fryer racks lightly.
10. Preheat the air fryer to 390°F.
11. Take out the mozzarella sticks from the freezer and once more, place into the whisked egg, and then into the mixture of the spices and crumbs. Once you are done, transfer them to the air fryer in batches if they cannot all fit into the rack.
12. Set the timer to 7-10 minutes and cook until you have crispy, golden brown mozzarella sticks.
13. Serve with marinara or any sauce of your choice.

Nutrition

Calories 113 | Fat 11 g | Protein 36 g | Sugar 2 g

112. Air Fryer Vegan Fried Ravioli

⏰ Prep Time 5 m | ⏱ Cooking Time 10 m | 2 Servings

Ingredients

- ¼ cup of Panko bread crumbs
- ½ teaspoons of dried basil
- 1 teaspoon of your favorite nutritional yeast flakes
- Pinch of pepper and small salt to taste
- ¼ cup of aquafaba liquid from the can or you can use other beans
- ½ teaspoon of garlic powder
- ½ teaspoon of dried oregano
- ¼ cup of marinara to dip
- 4 ounces of thawed vegan ravioli

Directions

1. Combine the nutritional yeast flakes, dried oregano, salt, pepper, dried basil, garlic powder, and panko bread crumbs on a plate or a clean surface.
2. Put your aquafaba in a separate bowl.
3. Carefully dip the ravioli in the aquafaba, and shake off the excess liquid.
4. After that, dredge it in the bread crumbs mixture while making sure that your ravioli is well covered.
5. Then, move the ravioli into the air fryer basket.
6. Do these steps for all the ravioli you want to cook.
7. Make sure to space the ravioli well in the air fryer basket to ensure that they can turn brown evenly.
8. Then go on to spritz your ravioli with cooking spray in the air fryer basket.
9. Set your air fryer to 390F.
10. Cook for 7 minutes and carefully turn each ravioli on their sides. Try as much as possible not to shake the baskets as you will waste the bread crumbs. After turning, proceed to cook for 2 more minutes.
11. Your ravioli is ready to eat. Make sure to serve with warm marinara as a dipping.
12. Save your leftovers in the refrigerator and reheat when you are ready to eat.

Nutrition

Calories 321 | Fat 2 g | Protein 15 g | Sugar 4 g

113. Air Fryer Veg Pizza

⏱ Prep Time 10 m | ⏱ Cooking Time 10 m | 4 Servings

Ingredients

- Pizza
- Pizza sauce
- Olives (or other veg toppings of your choice)
- Cheese
- Basil
- Pepper flakes

Directions

1. If you are just fetching the pizza out of the freezer, you might want to warm it. Set the air fryer to 350°F.
2. Once warm, top the pizza with the pizza sauce.
3. Add cheese to the pizza.
4. Add olives to the pizza.
5. Arrange the pizza carefully on the air fryer rack.

(NOTE: you can also set your dough into the air fryer rack before adding the toppings to prevent spills)

6. Preheat the air fryer to 350°F and spray air fryer rack with oil.
7. Set the timer to 5-7 minutes and cook until the cheese is melted.
8. Once cooked, let the cheese set on pizza by waiting for about 2-3 minutes before cutting.
9. Serve warm while topping it with basil and pepper flakes.

Nutrition

Calories 409 | Fat 18 g | Protein 13 g | Sugar 8 g

114. Air Fryer Buffalo Cauliflower – Onion Dip

⏱ Prep Time 10 m | ⏱ Cooking Time 12 m | 2 Servings

Ingredients

- ¾ head of cauliflower
- ¾ cup of buffalo sauce
- Seasoning and spice: garlic powder (1½ tsp.) and salt (to taste)
- Creamy dipping sauce: French onion dip (or any sauce of your choice)
- Celery
- 3 tbsp. olive oil

Directions

1. Cut the head of cauliflower into tiny florets into a big bowl.
2. Add and mix the cauliflower with the buffalo sauce and the rest of the ingredients apart from the dip sauce and celery sticks.
3. Grease the air fryer rack lightly.
4. Preheat the air fryer to 375°F.
5. Transfer the well-mixed cauliflower to the air fryer in batches if they cannot all fit into the rack.
6. Set the timer to 10-12 minutes and cook until the cauliflower florets are tender and browned a bit.
7. Serve warm with the celery sticks and dipping sauce of your choice. In my case, french onion dip.

Nutrition

Calories 265 | Fat 6 g | Protein 20 g | Sugar 6 g

115. Air Fryer Low Sodium Baked Apple

⏰ Prep Time 15 m | ⏱ Cooking Time 20 m | 2 Servings

Ingredients

- 2 apples
- Oats (as a topping)
- 3 tsp. melted margarine/butter
- ½ tsp. cinnamon
- ½ tsp. nutmeg powder
- 4 tbsp. raisins
- ½ cup of water

Directions

1. Wash and dry apples.
2. Slice the apples in two and use a spoon or knife to cut out some of the flesh.
3. Add the melted margarine, cinnamon, nutmeg powder, chopped raisins, and oats into a small bowl and mix.
4. Preheat the air fryer to 350°F.
5. Place the apples into the drip pan at the bottom of the air fryer.
6. Put the mixture into the center of the apples using a spoon.
7. Pour water into the pan.
8. Set the timer to 15-20 minutes for it to bake till apples are tender and fillings are crisp and browned.
9. Cover the fillings with foil if they seem to be browning quickly.
10. Serve warm and enjoy.

Nutrition

Calories 134 | Fat 7 g | Protein 41 g | Sugar 10 g

116. Vegan Air Fryer Eggplant Parmesan Recipe

⏰ Prep Time 15 m | ⏱ Cooking Time 20 m | 4 Servings

Ingredients

- 2 eggplants
- 1 cup whole wheat bread crumbs
- 1 cup flour
- 1 cup almond milk
- 4 tbsp. vegan parmesan
- Spices: onion powder, pepper, garlic powder, and salt (to taste)
- Sauce: marinara
- Toppings: 1 cup mozzarella shreds

Directions

1. Wash and dry eggplants.
2. Cut into slices.
3. Sieve flour to remove air bubbles into a bowl.
4. Mix whole wheat bread crumbs with vegan parmesan, onion powder, pepper, garlic powder, and salt together into a bowl.
5. Take the slices and dip into flour to be coated, then into the almond milk, and lastly into the mixture of vegan parmesan and spices.
6. Preheat air fryer at 375°F.
7. Place eggplant slices into the air fryer rack.
8. Set the timer to 15-20 minutes, pressing the "Rotate" so that you can turn the slices halfway through.
9. Once golden brown on both sides, top with marinara and the mozzarella shreds and air fry for about 1-2 minutes to melt.
10. Serve warm and enjoy with pasta or any meal of your choice.

Nutrition

Calories 300 | Fat 6 g | Protein 22 g | Sugar 11 g

117. Vegan Cheese Samosa

⏱ Prep Time 20 m | ⏱ Cooking Time 10 m | 3 Servings

Ingredients

For the Samosa:

- ½ tablespoon of pure olive oil
- ¼ cup of water
- 1 package of Samosa pastry sheet

For the Cheese:

- 1 ½ tablespoon of your favorite nutritional yeast
- ½ teaspoon of sea salt

- 1 ½ cup of water
- ¼ cup of raw cashew. It is best if you preboil for 9 minutes
- 2 ½ tablespoon and Tapioca starch (Don't use any other thickener apart from Tapioca, it would yield undesirable results.)
- ½ teaspoon of apple cider vinegar

Directions

1. Use your blender to blend all the cheese ingredients using the "high" option until the mixture is smooth.

2. Transfer the blended mixture into a saucepan then heat on medium temperature. Use a spatula to continuously stir while it cooks.

3. Your mixture will turn into a big mass of cheese at about 4 minutes and you will usually see the process start by the formation of clumps.

4. Cook for additional seconds to make sure it is well done.

5. Put it in the fridge to ensure that it cools before handling. This will take about 20 minutes.

6. After this, place a Samosa pastry sheet on your cutting board and start adding water slightly using a clean pastry brush. This is to make sure that the edges will stick together.

7. Then, add about 1-2 teaspoons of the cheese mixture to the far right corner. Using the bottom right, carefully fold the pastry over the filling to form a triangular shape.

8. Take the top right point of the triangle and proceed to fold horizontally. You should do the previous two steps till you have a triangular-shaped parcel, with the final flap sealed.

9. Repeat this till all your samosa flaps are used.

10. Brush each Samosa with the pastry brush using the pure olive oil. Do this for each side.

11. Place 4-6 parcels of the Samosa in your Air Fryer basket.

12. Cook at 385F for 7-9 minutes until it is crisp and well done.

13. Freeze the leftovers.

Nutrition

Calories 543 | Fat 34 g | Protein 10 g | Sugar 0 g

118. Delicious Air Fryer Potato Chips

⏱ Prep Time 5 m | ⏱ Cooking Time 15 m | 3 Servings

Ingredients

- Grapeseed oil cooking spray or any other cooking spray of your choice.
- Seasonings of choice.
- Pinch of sea salt according to your taste
- 2 medium-sized Russet potato.

Directions

1. Slice your potato after removing the outer cover. Make sure to slice into thin, cylindrical shapes.
2. Use a paper towel to remove as much water from the thin potato slice. Don't do this too hard.
3. Use a teaspoon to add the seasoning of your choice uniformly to the potato slices.
4. Then, spray your Air Fryer Basket with oil spray.
5. Place the sliced potatoes in a single layer inside the basket, you can do this in batches.
6. Go on to spray the top of the potato batches with grape seed oil spray and sprinkle with your sea salt.
7. Cook in your Air Fryer at 450F until the edges of the potatoes become golden brown.
8. Depending on how thin your potato slices are, this should take about 15 minutes to cook in your Air Fryer.
9. Remove the crispy chips from your Fryer and let it cool down before eating.
10. You can store leftovers in the fridge.

Nutrition

Calories 532 | Fat 21 g | Protein 45 g | Sugar 4 g

Fish and Seafood Recipes

119. Prawn Momo's Recipe

⏰ Prep Time 15 m | ⏱ Cooking Time 25 m | 4 Servings

Ingredients

- 1 ½ cup all-purpose flour
- ½ tsp. salt
- 5 tbsp. water

For filling:

- 2 cups minced prawn

- 2 tbsp. oil
- 2 tsp. ginger-garlic paste
- 2 tsp. soya sauce
- 2 tsp. vinegar

Directions

1. Squeeze the dough and cover it with plastic wrap and set aside. Next, cook the ingredients for the filling and try to ensure that the prawn is covered well with the sauce. Roll the dough and cut it into a square.

2. Place the filling in the center. Now, wrap the dough to cover the filling and pinch the edges together. Preheat the Breville smart oven at 200° F for 5 minutes. Place the wontons in the fry basket and close it. Let them cook at the same temperature for another 20 minutes. Recommended sides are chili sauce or ketchup.

Nutrition

Calories 300 | Fat 11 g | Protein 35 g | Sugar 6 g

120. Fish Club Classic Sandwich

⏰ Prep Time 10 m | ⏱ Cooking Time 20 m | 3 Servings

Ingredients

- 2 slices of white bread
- 1 tbsp. softened butter
- 1 tin tuna
- 1 small capsicum

For Barbeque Sauce:

- ¼ tbsp. Worcestershire sauce
- ½ tsp. olive oil
- ½ flake garlic crushed

- ¼ cup chopped onion
- ¼ tsp. mustard powder
- ½ tbsp. sugar
- ¼ tbsp. red chili sauce
- 1 tbsp. tomato ketchup
- ½ cup water.
- Salt and black pepper to taste

Directions

1. Remove the edges of the sliced bread. Now cut the slices horizontally. Cook the ingredients for the sauce and wait till it thickens. Now, add the fish to the sauce and stir till it obtains the flavors. Roast the capsicum and peel the skin off. Cut the capsicum into slices.

2. Mix the ingredients and apply it to the bread slices. Pre-heat the Breville smart oven for 5 minutes at 300 Fahrenheit.

3. Open the basket of the Fryer and place the prepared classic sandwiches in it such that no two classic sandwiches are touching each other. Now keep the fryer at 250 degrees for around 15 minutes. Turn the classic sandwiches in between the cooking process to cook both slices. Serve the classic sandwiches with tomato ketchup or mint sauce.

Nutrition

Calories 232 | Fat 22 g | Protein 25 g | Sugar 5 g

121. Prawn Fried Baked Pastry

⏰ Prep Time 15 m | ⏱ Cooking Time 35 m | 4 Servings

Ingredients

- 1 ½ cup all-purpose flour
- 2 tbsp. unsalted butter
- 2 green chilies that are finely chopped or mashed
- Add a lot of water to make the dough stiff and firm
- A pinch of salt to taste
- 1 lb. prawn
- ¼ cup boiled peas
- ½ tsp. cumin

- 1 tsp. coarsely crushed coriander
- 1 dry red chili broken into pieces
- A small amount of salt (to taste)
- ½ tsp. dried mango powder
- 1 tsp. powdered ginger
- ½ tsp. red chili powder
- 1-2 tbsp. coriander

Directions

1. You will first need to make the outer covering. In a large bowl, add the flour, butter, and enough water to knead it into the stiff dough. Transfer this to a container and leave it to rest for five minutes. Place a pan on medium flame and add the oil. Roast the mustard seeds and once roasted, add the coriander seeds and the chopped dry red chilies. Add all the dry ingredients for the filling and mix the ingredients well.

2. Add a little water and continue to mix the ingredients. Make small balls from the dough and wrap them. Cut the wrapped dough in half and spread a little water on the edges to help you fold the halves into a cone. Add the filling to the cone and close the samosa. Preheat the Breville Smart Oven for about 5 to 6 minutes at 300 Fahrenheit. Place all the samosas in the frying pan and close the basket properly.

3. Keep the Breville Smart Oven at 200 degrees for another 20 to 25 minutes. Around half point, open the basket and turn the samosas for even cooking. After that, fry at 250 degrees for about 10 minutes to give them the desired golden-brown color. Serve hot. Recommended sides are tamarind or mint sauce.

Nutrition

Calories 132 | Fat 1 g | Protein 15 g | Sugar 9 g

122. Fish Spicy Lemon Kebab

⏰ Prep Time 10 m | ⏰ Cooking Time 25 m | 3 Servings

Ingredients

- 1 lb. boneless fish roughly chopped
- 3 onions chopped
- 5 green chilies-roughly chopped
- 1 ½ tbsp. ginger paste
- 1 ½ tsp garlic paste
- 1 ½ tsp salt
- 3 tsp lemon juice
- 2 tsp garam masala
- 4 tbsp. chopped coriander
- 3 tbsp. cream
- 2 tbsp. coriander powder
- 4 tbsp. fresh mint chopped
- 3 tbsp. chopped capsicum
- 3 eggs
- 2 ½ tbsp. white sesame seeds

Directions

1. Take all the ingredients mentioned under the first heading and mix them in a bowl. Grind them thoroughly to make a smooth paste. Take the eggs in a different bowl and beat them. Add a pinch of salt and leave them aside. Take a flat plate and in it, mix the sesame seeds and breadcrumbs. Mold the mixture of fish into small balls and flatten them into round and flat kebabs. Dip these kebabs in the egg and salt mixture and then in the mixture of breadcrumbs and sesame seeds. Leave these kebabs in the fridge for an hour or so to set.

2. Preheat the Breville smart oven at 160 degrees Fahrenheit for around 5 minutes. Place the kebabs in the basket and let them cook for another 25 minutes at the same temperature. Turn the kebabs over in between the cooking process to get a uniform cook. Serve the kebabs with mint sauce.

Nutrition

Calories 432 | Fat 3 g | Protein 22 g | Sugar 1 g

123. Fish Oregano Fingers

⏲ Prep Time 10 m | ⏲ Cooking Time 25 m | 5 Servings

Ingredients

- ½ lb. firm white fish fillet cut into Oregano Fingers
- 1 tbsp. lemon juice
- 2 cups of dry breadcrumbs
- 1 cup oil for frying
- 1 ½ tbsp. ginger-garlic paste
- 3 tbsp. lemon juice

- 2 tsp salt
- 1 ½ tsp pepper powder
- 1 tsp red chili
- 3 eggs
- 5 tbsp. corn flour
- 2 tsp tomato ketchup

Directions

1. Rub a little lemon juice on the oregano fingers and set aside. Wash the fish after an hour and pat dry. Make the marinade and transfer the oregano fingers into the marinade. Allow them to dry on a plate for fifteen minutes. Now cover the oregano fingers with the crumbs and set aside to dry for fifteen minutes.

2. Preheat the Breville smart oven at 160 degrees Fahrenheit for 5 minutes or so. Keep the fish in the fry basket now and close it properly.

3. Let the oregano fingers cook at the same temperature for another 25 minutes. In between the cooking process, toss the fish once in a while to avoid burning the food. Serve either with tomato ketchup or chili sauce. Mint sauce also works well with the fish.

Nutrition

Calories 234 | Fat 3 g | Protein 35 g | Sugar 0 g

124. Prawn Grandma's Easy to Cook Wontons

⏲ Prep Time 5 m | ⏲ Cooking Time 20 m | 3 Servings

Ingredients

- 1 ½ cup all-purpose flour
- ½ tsp. salt
- 5 tbsp. water
- 2 cups minced prawn

- 2 tbsp. oil
- 2 tsp. ginger-garlic paste
- 2 tsp. soya sauce
- 2 tsp. vinegar

Directions

1. Squeeze out the dough and cover it with plastic wrap and set it aside. Then cook the ingredients for the filling and try to make sure the shrimp are well coated with the sauce. Roll out the dough and place the filling in the center.

2. Now, roll the dough to cover the filling and bring the edges together. Preheat the Breville Smart Oven to 200 ° F for 5 minutes. Place the wontons in the pan and close it. Let them cook at equal temperature for another 20 minutes. Recommended sides are chili sauce or ketchup.

Nutrition

Calories 423 | Fat 20 g | Protein 20 g | Sugar 2 g

125. Tuna Sandwich

⏱ Prep Time 5 m | ⏱ Cooking Time 15 m | 4 Servings

Ingredients

- 2 slices of white bread
- 1 tbsp. softened butter
- 1 tin tuna
- 1 small capsicum
- For Barbeque Sauce:
- ¼ tbsp. Worcestershire sauce
- ½ tsp. olive oil
- ¼ tsp. mustard powder
- ½ flake garlic crushed
- ¼ cup chopped onion
- ½ tbsp. sugar
- 1 tbsp. tomato ketchup
- ½ cup water.
- ¼ tbsp. red chili sauce
- Salt and black pepper to taste

Directions

1. Remove the edges of the slices of bread. Now cut the slices horizontally. Cook the ingredients for the sauce and wait till it thickens. Now, add the lamb to the sauce and stir till it obtains the flavors. Roast the capsicum and peel the skin off. Cut the capsicum into slices. Mix the ingredients and apply it to the bread slices.

2. Pre-heat the Breville smart oven for 5 minutes at 300 Fahrenheit. Open the basket of the Fryer and place the prepared classic sandwiches in it such that no two classic sandwiches are touching each other. Now keep the fryer at 250 degrees for around 15 minutes. Turn the classic sandwiches in between the cooking process to cook both slices. Serve the classic sandwiches with tomato ketchup or mint sauce.

Nutrition

Calories 460 | Fat 1 g | Protein 11 g | Sugar 5 g

126. Salmon Tandoor

⏰ Prep Time 10 m | ⏰ Cooking Time 20 m | 5 Servings

Ingredients

- 2 lb. boneless salmon filets

1st Marinade:

- 3 tbsp. vinegar or lemon juice
- 2 or 3 tsp. paprika
- 1 tsp. black pepper
- 1 tsp. salt
- 3 tsp. ginger-garlic paste

2nd Marinade:

- 1 cup yogurt
- 4 tsp. tandoori masala
- 2 tbsp. dry fenugreek leaves
- 1 tsp. black salt
- 1 tsp. chat masala
- 1 tsp. garam masala powder
- 1 tsp. red chili powder
- 1 tsp. salt
- 3 drops of red color

Directions

1. Make the first marinade and soak the fileted salmon in it for four hours. While this is happening, make the second marinade and soak the salmon in it overnight to let the flavors blend. Preheat the Breville smart oven at 160 degrees Fahrenheit for 5 minutes.

2. Put the oregano fingers in the pan and close it. Let them cook at an equal temperature for another 15 minutes or so. Toss the oregano fingers well so that they are well cooked. Serve with mint sauce.

Nutrition

Calories 187 | Fat 2 g | Protein 30 g | Sugar 0 g

127. Carp Best Homemade Croquette

⏰ Prep Time 15 m | ⏰ Cooking Time 25 m | 3 Servings

Ingredients

- 1 lb. Carp filets
- 3 onions chopped
- 5 green chilies-roughly chopped
- 1 ½ tbsp. ginger paste
- 1 ½ tsp garlic paste
- 1 ½ tsp salt
- 3 tsp lemon juice
- 2 tsp garam masala

- 4 tbsp. chopped coriander
- 3 tbsp. cream
- 2 tbsp. coriander powder
- 4 tbsp. fresh mint chopped
- 3 tbsp. chopped capsicum
- 3 eggs
- 2 ½ tbsp. white sesame seeds

Directions

1. Take all the ingredients mentioned under the first heading and mix them in a bowl. Grind them thoroughly to make a smooth paste. Take the eggs in a different bowl and beat them. Add a pinch of salt and leave them aside. Mold the fish mixture into small balls and flatten them into round and flat Best Homemade Croquettes. Dip these croquettes in the egg and salt mixture and then in the mixture of breadcrumbs and sesame seeds.

2. Leave these croquettes in the fridge for an hour or so to set. Preheat the Breville smart oven at 160 degrees Fahrenheit for around 5 minutes. Place the croquettes in the basket and let them cook for another 25 minutes at the same temperature. Turn the croquettes over in between the cooking process to get a uniform cook. Serve the croquettes with mint sauce.

Nutrition

Calories 209 | Fat 4 g | Protein 49 g | Sugar 1g

128. Shrimp Momo's Recipe

⏰ Prep Time 10 m | ⏰ Cooking Time 20 m | 7 Servings

Ingredients

- 1 ½ cup all-purpose flour
- ½ tsp. salt
- 5 tbsp. water

For filling:

- 2 cups minced shrimp

- 2 tbsp. oil
- 2 tsp. ginger-garlic paste
- 2 tsp. soya sauce
- 2 tsp. vinegar

Directions

1. Squeeze out the dough and cover it with plastic wrap and set it aside. Then cook the ingredients for the filling and try to make sure the shrimp are well coated with the sauce. Roll up the dough and cut it into squares. Place the filling in the center.

2. Now, roll the dough to cover the filling and bring the edges together. Preheat the Breville Smart Oven to 200 ° F for 5 minutes. Place the wontons in the pan and close it. Let them cook at an equal temperature for another 20 minutes. Recommended sides are chili sauce or ketchup.

Nutrition

Calories 103 | Fat 0 g | Protein 34 g | Sugar 11 g

129. Salmon Fries

⏰ Prep Time 5 m | ⏰ Cooking Time 15 m | 3 Servings

Ingredients

- 1 lb. boneless salmon filets
- 2 cup dry breadcrumbs
- 2 tsp. oregano
- 2 tsp. red chili flakes
- 1 ½ tbsp. ginger-garlic paste
- 4 tbsp. lemon juice

- 2 tsp. salt
- 1 tsp. pepper powder
- 1 tsp. red chili powder
- 6 tbsp. corn flour
- 4 eggs

Directions

1. Mix every ingredient for the marinade and put the salmon fillets and leave to rest overnight. Mix the toast, oregano, and red chili flakes well and place the marinated oregano fingers in this mixture. Cover with cling film and leave until served.

2. Preheat the Breville smart oven to 160 degrees Fahrenheit for 5 minutes.

3. Put the oregano fingers in the pan and close it. Let them cook at an equal temperature for another 15 minutes or so. Toss the oregano fingers well so that they are well cooked.

Nutrition

Calories 300 | Fat 3 g | Protein 16 g | Sugar 2 g

130. Cheese Carp Fries

⏰ Prep Time 15 m | ⏰ Cooking Time 25 m | 4 Servings

Ingredients

- 1 lb. carp oregano fingers
- Ingredients for the marinade:
- 1 tbsp. olive oil
- 1 tsp. mixed herbs
- ½ tsp. red chili flakes

- A pinch of salt to taste
- 1 tbsp. lemon juice
- For the garnish:
- 1 cup melted cheddar cheese

Directions

1. Take all the ingredients mentioned in the heading "For the marinade" and mix well. Cook the oregano fingers and dip them in the marinade.

2. Preheat the Breville smart oven for about 5 minutes at 300 Fahrenheit. Take the basket out of the fryer and place

the tent in it. Close the basket. Now keep the fryer at 220 Fahrenheit for 20 to 25 minutes.

3. Between the process, toss the potatoes two or three times so they are cooked through. Towards the rare end of the cooking process (the last 2 minutes or so), sprinkle the melted cheddar cheese over the potatoes and serve hot.

Nutrition

Calories 502 | Fat 22 g | Protein 40 g | Sugar: 14 g

131. Oyster Club Sandwich

⏰ Prep Time 10 m | ⏱ Cooking Time 15 m | 4 Servings

Ingredients

- 2 slices of white bread
- 1 tbsp. softened butter
- ½ lb. shelled oyster
- 1 small capsicum

For Barbeque Sauce:

- ¼ tbsp. Worcestershire sauce
- ½ tsp. olive oil
- ½ flake garlic crushed

- ¼ cup chopped onion
- ¼ tsp. mustard powder
- 1 tbsp. tomato ketchup
- ½ tbsp. sugar
- ¼ tbsp. red chili sauce
- ½ cup water.
- Salt and black pepper to taste

Directions

1. Remove the edges of the slices of bread. Now cut the slices horizontally. Cook the ingredients for the sauce and wait till it thickens. Now, add the oyster to the sauce and stir till it obtains the flavors.

2. Roast the capsicum and peel the skin off. Cut the capsicum into slices. Mix all ingredients together and apply it to the bread slices. Pre-heat the Breville smart oven for 5 minutes at 300 Fahrenheit. Open the basket of the Fryer and place the prepared classic sandwiches in it such that no two classic sandwiches are touching each other. Now keep the fryer at 250 degrees for around 15 minutes.

3. Turn the classic sandwiches in between the cooking process to cook both slices. Serve the Classic Sandwiches with tomato ketchup or mint sauce.

Nutrition

Calories 407 | Fat 10 g | Protein 31 g | Sugar 11 g

132. Lobster Grandma's Easy to Cook Wontons

⏰ Prep Time 10 m | ⏱ Cooking Time 20 m | 4 Servings

Ingredients

- 1 ½ cup all-purpose flour
- ½ tsp. salt
- 5 tbsp. water
- For filling:
- 2 cups minced lobster

- 2 tbsp. oil
- 2 tsp. ginger-garlic paste
- 2 tsp. soya sauce
- 2 tsp. vinegar

Directions

1. Squeeze out the dough and cover it with plastic wrap and set it aside. Then cook the ingredients for the filling and try to make sure the lobster is well coated with the sauce.

2. Roll out the dough and place the filling in the center. Now, roll the dough to cover the filling and bring the edges together.

3. Preheat the Breville Smart Oven to 200 ° F for 5 minutes. Place the wontons in the pan and close it. Let them cook at an equal temperature for another 20 minutes. Recommended sides are chili sauce or ketchup.

Nutrition

Calories 600 | Fat 13 g | Protein 21 g | Sugar 9 g

133. Seafood Pizza

⏰ Prep Time 10 m | ⏱ Cooking Time 22 m | 4 Servings

Ingredients

- One pizza base
- Grated pizza cheese (mozzarella cheese preferably) for topping
- Some pizza topping sauce
- Use cooking oil for brushing and topping purposes

Ingredients for topping:

- 2 onions chopped

- 2 cups mixed seafood
- 2 capsicums chopped
- 2 tomatoes that have been deseeded and chopped
- 1 tbsp. (optional) mushrooms/corns
- 2 tsp. pizza seasoning
- Some cottage cheese that has been cut into small cubes (optional)

Directions

1. Put the pizza base in a pre-heated Breville smart oven for around 5 minutes. (Preheated to 340 Fahrenheit). Take out the base. Pour some pizza sauce on top of the base at the center. Using a spoon, spread the sauce over the base making sure that you leave some gap around the circumference. Grate some mozzarella cheese and sprinkle it over the sauce layer. Take all the vegetables and the seafood and mix them in a bowl. Add some oil and seasoning.

2. Also, add some salt and pepper according to taste. Mix them properly. Put this topping over the layer of cheese on the pizza. Now sprinkle some more grated cheese and pizza seasoning on top of this layer. Preheat the Breville smart oven at 250 Fahrenheit for around 5 minutes.

3. Open the fry basket and place the pizza inside. Close the basket and keep the fryer at 170 degrees for another 10 minutes. If you feel that it is undercooked, you may put it at the same temperature for another 2 minutes or so.

Nutrition

Calories 116 | Fat 23 g | Protein 29 g | Sugar 1 g

134. Crab Cakes

⏰ Prep Time 5 m | ⏱ Cooking Time 10 m | 4 Servings

Ingredients

- 8 ounces jumbo lump crabmeat
- 1 tablespoon Old Bay seasoning
- ⅓ cup bread crumbs
- ¼ cup diced red bell pepper
- ¼ cup diced green bell pepper

- 1 egg
- ¼ cup mayonnaise
- Juice of ½ lemon
- 1 teaspoon flour
- Cooking oil

Directions

1. In a bowl, combine the crab meat, Old Bay seasoning, bread crumbs, red bell pepper, green bell pepper, egg, mayo, and lemon juice. Mix gently to combine.

2. Form the mixture into 4 patties. Sprinkle ¼ teaspoon of flour on top of each patty.

3. Place the crab cakes in the air fryer. Spray them with cooking oil. Cook for 10 minutes.

4. Serve.

5. Ingredient tip: You can make your own crab seasoning using ¼ teaspoon of each of the following: celery salt, black pepper, red pepper flakes, and paprika.

Nutrition

Calories 176 | Fat 8g | Saturated Fat 1g | Cholesterol 101mg | Sodium 826mg | Carbohydrates 12g | Fiber 1g | Protein 15g

135. Cilantro-Lime Fried Shrimp

⏰ Prep Time 10 m | ⏰ Cooking Time 10 m | 4 Servings

Ingredients

- ½ cup chopped fresh cilantro
- Juice of 1 lime
- 1 pound of raw shrimp, deveined and peeled with tails on or off
- 1 egg
- ½ cup all-purpose flour
- ¾ cup bread crumbs
- Salt
- Pepper
- Cooking oil
- ½ cup cocktail sauce (optional)

Directions

1. Place the shrimp in a plastic bag. Add the cilantro and lime juice. Seal the bag. Shake to combine. Marinate in the refrigerator for 30 minutes.
2. In a small bowl, beat the egg. In another small bowl, place the flour. Place the crumbs of bread in a third small bowl, and season with salt and pepper to taste.
3. Spray cooking oil to the air fryer basket.
4. Remove the shrimp from the plastic bag. Wet each in the flour, then the egg, and then the bread crumbs.
5. Place the shrimp in the air fryer. It is okay to stack them. Spray the shrimp with cooking oil. Cook for 4 minutes.
6. Open the air fryer and flip the shrimp. I recommend flipping individually instead of shaking to keep the breading intact. Cook for another 4 minutes, or until crisp.
7. Cool before serving. Serve with cocktail sauce if desired.
8. Substitution tip: You can reduce the number of calories and fat in this recipe by substituting an egg white for the whole egg.
9. Preparation tip: If using frozen shrimp, place the shrimp in a large bowl of cold water to thaw. Let the shrimp soak for 15 minutes.

Nutrition

Calories 254 | Fat 4g | Saturated Fat 1g | Cholesterol 221mg | Sodium 334mg | Carbohydrates 27g | Fiber 1g | Protein 29g

136. Salmon Croquettes

⏰ Prep Time 5 m | ⏰ Cooking Time 15 m | 6 Servings

Ingredients

- 1 (14.75-ounce) can Alaskan pink salmon, drained and bones removed
- 1 egg, beaten
- ½ cup bread crumbs
- 2 scallions, diced
- 1 teaspoon garlic powder
- Salt
- Pepper
- Cooking oil

Directions

1. In a large bowl, combine the salmon, beaten egg, bread crumbs, and scallions. Season with the garlic powder and salt and pepper to taste.
2. Form the mixture into 6 patties.
3. Place the croquettes in the air fryer. It is okay to stack them. Spray the croquettes with cooking oil. Cook for 7 minutes.
4. Open the air fryer and flip the patties. Cook for an additional 3 to 4 minutes, or until golden brown.

Nutrition

Calories 142 | Fat 6g | Saturated Fat 1g | Cholesterol 58mg | Sodium 135mg | Carbohydrates 7g | Fiber 1g | Protein 16g

137. Beer-Battered Fish and Chips

⏱ Prep Time 5 m | ⏱ Cooking Time 30 m | 4 Servings

Ingredients

- 2 eggs
- 1 cup malty beer, such as Pabst Blue Ribbon
- 1 cup all-purpose flour
- ½ cup cornstarch
- 1 teaspoon garlic powder
- Salt
- Pepper
- Cooking oil
- 4 (4-ounce) cod fillets

Directions

1. Beat the eggs with the beer. In another medium bowl, combine the flour and cornstarch, and season with the garlic powder and salt and pepper to taste.
2. Spray cooking oil to the air fryer basket.
3. Dip each cod fillet in the flour and cornstarch mixture and then in the egg and beer mixture. Dip the cod in the flour and cornstarch a second time.
4. Place the cod in the air fryer. Do not stack. Cook in batches. Spray with cooking oil. Cook for 8 minutes.
5. Open the air fryer and flip the cod. Cook for an additional 7 minutes.
6. Remove the cooked cod from the air fryer, then repeat steps 4 and 5 for the remaining fillets.
7. Serve with Classic French Fries or prepare air-fried frozen fries. Frozen fries will need to be cooked for 18 to 20 minutes at 400°F.
8. Cool before serving.

Nutrition

Calories 325 | Fat 4g | Saturated Fat 1g | Cholesterol 137mg | Sodium 144mg | Carbohydrates 41g | Fiber 1g | Protein 26g

138. Firecracker Shrimp

⏰ Prep Time 10 m | ⏱ Cooking Time 10 m | 4 Servings

Ingredients

For the shrimp:

- 1-pound raw shrimp, peeled and deveined
- Salt
- Pepper
- 1 egg
- ½ cup all-purpose flour

- ¾ cup panko bread crumbs
- Cooking oil

For the firecracker sauce:

- ⅓ cup sour cream
- 2 tablespoons Sriracha
- ¼ cup sweet chili sauce

Directions

To make the shrimp:

1. Add the shrimp with pepper and salt to taste.
2. In a small bowl, beat the egg.
3. In another small bowl, place the flour. In another small bowl, add the panko bread crumbs.
4. Spray cooking oil to the air fryer basket.
5. Dip the shrimp in the flour, then the egg, and then the bread crumbs.
6. Place the shrimp in the fryer basket. It is okay to stack them. Spray the shrimp with cooking oil. Cook for 4 minutes.

7. Open the air fryer and flip the shrimp. I recommend flipping individually instead of shaking to keep the breading intact.
8. Cook for another 4 minutes or until crisp.

To make the firecracker sauce:

9. While the shrimp is cooking, make the firecracker sauce: In a small bowl, combine the sour cream, Sriracha, and sweet chili sauce. Mix well.
10. Serve with the shrimp.

Substitution tip: In place of sour cream, use nonfat plain Greek yogurt. This saves calories and fat while providing 5.5 grams of additional protein.

Nutrition

Calories 266 | Fat 6g | Saturated Fat 3g | Cholesterol 229mg | Sodium 393mg | Carbohydrates 23g | Fiber 1g | Protein 27g

139. Coconut Shrimp

⏰ Prep Time 10 m | ⏰ Cooking Time 10 m | 4 Servings

Ingredients

- 1-pound raw shrimp, peeled and deveined
- 1 egg
- ¼ cup all-purpose flour
- ⅓ cup shredded unsweetened coconut
- ¼ cup panko bread crumbs
- Salt
- Pepper
- Cooking oil

Directions

1. Dry the shrimp with paper towels.
2. In a small bowl, beat the egg. In another small bowl, place the flour. In a third small bowl, combine the coconut and panko bread crumbs, and season with salt and pepper to taste. Mix well.
3. Spray cooking oil to the air fryer basket.
4. Dip the shrimp in the flour, then the egg, and then the coconut and bread crumb mixture.
5. Place the shrimp in the air fryer. It is okay to stack them. Cook for 4 minutes.
6. Open the air fryer and flip the shrimp. I recommend flipping individually instead of shaking, which keeps the breading intact. Cook for another 4 minutes or until crisp.
7. Cool before serving.

Nutrition

Calories 182 | Fat 6g | Saturated Fat 3g | Cholesterol 246mg | Sodium 780mg | Carbohydrates 8g | Fiber 1g | Protein 24g

140. Spicy Shrimp Kebab

⏰ Prep Time 25 m | ⏰ Cooking Time 20 m | 4 Servings

Ingredients

- 1 ½ pounds jumbo shrimp, cleaned, shelled, and deveined
- 1-pound cherry tomatoes
- 2 tablespoons butter, melted
- 1 tablespoons sriracha sauce
- Sea salt and ground black pepper
- 1/2 teaspoon dried oregano
- 1/2 teaspoon dried basil
- 1 teaspoon dried parsley flakes
- 1/2 teaspoon marjoram
- 1/2 teaspoon mustard seeds

Directions

1. Toss all elements in a mixing bowl until the shrimp and tomatoes are covered on all sides.
2. Let the wooden skewers be soaked in water for 15 minutes.
3. Thread the jumbo shrimp and cherry tomatoes onto skewers. Cook in the preheated air fryer at a temperature of 400 degrees F for 5 minutes, working with batches.

Nutrition

Calories 247 | Fat 8.4g | Carbohydrates 6g | Protein 36.4g | Sugar 3.5g | Fiber 1.8g

141. Lemon-Pepper Tilapia with Garlic Aioli

⏰ Prep Time 5 m | ⏱ Cooking Time 15 m | 4 Servings

Ingredients

For the tilapia:

- 4 tilapia fillets
- 1 tablespoon extra-virgin olive oil
- 1 teaspoon paprika
- 1 teaspoon garlic powder
- 1 teaspoon dried basil
- Lemon-pepper seasoning (such as McCormick Perfect Pinch Lemon & Pepper Seasoning)

For the garlic aioli:

- 2 garlic cloves, minced
- 1 tablespoon mayonnaise
- 1 teaspoon extra-virgin olive oil
- Juice of ½ lemon
- Salt
- Pepper

Directions

1. To make the tilapia:
2. Coat the fish with the olive oil. Season with the paprika, garlic powder, dried basil, and lemon-pepper seasoning.
3. Place the fish in the air fryer. It is okay to stack the fish. Cook for 8 minutes.
4. Open the fryer and flip the fish. Cook for an additional 7 minutes.
5. To make the garlic aioli:
6. In a bowl, put together the garlic, mayonnaise, olive oil, lemon juice, and salt and pepper to taste. Whisk well to combine.
7. Serve alongside the fish.

Variation tip: This recipe can be made gluten-free by using gluten-free mayonnaise; be sure to check the label.

Ingredient tip: You can make your own lemon-pepper seasoning using the juice of ½ lemon and pepper to taste.

Preparation tip: If using frozen tilapia, the best way to thaw it is in a covered bowl in the refrigerator overnight. You can keep the fish in a sealed plastic bag as well and submerge the bag in cold water for 15 minutes or till thawed.

Nutrition

Calories 155 | Total fat: 7g | Saturated fat: 1g | Cholesterol: 56mg | Sodium: 107mg | Carbohydrates: 2g | Fiber: 0g | Protein: 21g

142. Blackened Shrimp

☺ Prep Time 5 m | ☺ Cooking Time 10 m | 4 Servings

Ingredients

- 1-pound raw shrimp, peeled and deveined
- 1 teaspoon paprika
- ½ teaspoon dried oregano
- ½ teaspoon cayenne pepper
- Juice of ½ lemon
- Salt
- Pepper
- Cooking oil

Directions

1. Put the shrimp in a sealable plastic bag then add the paprika, oregano, cayenne pepper, lemon juice, and salt and pepper to taste. Seal the bag. Shake well to combine.
2. Spray a grill pan or the air fryer basket with cooking oil.
3. Place the shrimp in the air fryer. It is okay to stack the shrimp. Cook for 4 minutes.
4. Open the air fryer then after that, shake the basket. Heat for an additional of 3 to 4 minutes, or til the shrimp has blackened.
5. Cool before serving.

Variation tip: This shrimp is delicious over a green salad with avocado. Dress it with a simple cilantro-lime vinaigrette made from chopped fresh cilantro, lime juice, and olive oil.

Nutrition

Calories 101 | Total fat: 2g | Saturated fat: 2g | Cholesterol: 168mg | Sodium: 759mg | Carbohydrates: 0g | Fiber: 0g | Protein: 21g

143. Fried Catfish Nuggets

☺ Prep Time 5 m | ☺ Cooking Time 40 m | 4 Servings

Ingredients

- 1-pound catfish fillets, cut into 1-inch chunks
- ½ cup seasoned fish fry breading mix (such as Louisiana Fish Fry)
- Cooking oil

Directions

1. Rinse and thoroughly dry the catfish. Pour the seasoned fish fry breading mix into a sealable plastic bag and add the catfish. (You may need to use two bags depending on the size of your nuggets.) Seal the bag and shake to coat the fish with breading evenly.
2. Spray cooking oil to the air fryer basket.
3. Transfer the catfish nuggets to the air fryer. Do not overcrowd the basket. You may need to cook the nuggets in two batches. Spray the nuggets with cooking oil. Cook for 10 minutes.
4. Open the air fryer then after that, shake the basket. Cook for an additional of 8 to 10 minutes, or till the fish is crisp.
5. If necessary, remove the cooked catfish nuggets from the air fryer, then repeat steps 3 and 4 for the remaining fish.
6. Cool before serving.

Ingredient tip: You may be able to purchase catfish nuggets at the fish counter of your grocery store. It's worth asking!

Cooking tip: Open the air fryer and check in on the fish a few times throughout the cooking process. When the fish has turned golden brown on both sides, it has finished cooking.

Nutrition

Calories 183 | Total fat: 9g | Saturated fat: 2g | Cholesterol: 56mg | Sodium: 199mg | Carbohydrates: 5g | Fiber: 0g | Protein: 19g

144. Cornmeal Shrimp Po'boy

⏰ Prep Time 10 m | ⏱ Cooking Time 10 m | 4 Servings

Ingredients

For the shrimp:

- 1-pound shrimp, peeled and deveined
- 1 egg
- ½ cup flour
- ¾ cup cornmeal
- Salt
- Pepper
- Cooking oil

For the remoulade:

- ½ cup mayonnaise

- 1 teaspoon mustard (I use Dijon)
- 1 teaspoon Worcestershire
- 1 teaspoon minced garlic
- Juice of ½ lemon
- 1 teaspoon Sriracha
- ½ teaspoon Creole seasoning

For the po'boys:

- 4 rolls
- 2 cups shredded lettuce
- 8 slices tomato

Directions

1. To make the shrimp:
2. Dry the shrimp with paper towels.
3. In a small bowl, beat the egg. In another small bowl, place the flour. Place the cornmeal in a third small bowl, and season with salt and pepper to taste.
4. Spray cooking oil to the air fryer basket.
5. Dip the shrimp in the flour, then the egg, and then the cornmeal.
6. Place the shrimp in the air fryer. Cook for 4 minutes. Open the basket and flip the shrimp. Cook for another 4 minutes, or till crisp.
7. To make the remoulade:
8. While the shrimp is cooking, in a small bowl, combine the mayonnaise, mustard, Worcestershire, garlic, lemon juice, Sriracha, and Creole seasoning. Mix well.
9. To make the po'boys:
10. Split the rolls and spread them with the remoulade.
11. Let the shrimp cool slightly before assembling the po'boys.
12. Fill each roll with a quarter of the shrimp, ½ cup of shredded lettuce, and 2 slices of tomato. Serve.

Nutrition

Calories 483 | Total fat: 15g | Saturated fat: 2g | Cholesterol: 229mg | Sodium: 690mg | Carbohydrates: 58g | Fiber: 6g | Protein: 32g

145. Crumbed Fish Fillets with Tarragon

⏱ Prep Time 25 m | ⏱ Cooking Time 20 m | 4 Servings

Ingredients

- 2 eggs, beaten
- 1 2 teaspoon tarragon
- 4 fish fillets, halved
- 2 tablespoons dry white wine

- 1/3 cup parmesan cheese, grated
- 1 teaspoon seasoned salt
- 1/3 teaspoon mixed peppercorns
- 1/2 teaspoon fennel seed

Directions

1. Add the parmesan cheese, salt, peppercorns, fennel seeds, and tarragon to your food processor; blitz for about 20 seconds.
2. Drizzle fish fillets with dry white wine. Dump the egg into a shallow dish.

3. Now, coat the fish fillets with the beaten egg on all sides; then, coat them with the seasoned cracker mix.
4. Air-fry at 345 degrees F for about 17 minutes.

Nutrition

305 calories | 17.7g fat | 6.3g Carbohydrates | 27.2g protein | 0.3g sugar | 0.1g fiber

146. Smoked and Creamed White Fish

⏱ Prep Time 20 m | ⏱ Cooking Time 15 m | 4 Servings

Ingredients

- 1/2 tablespoon yogurt
- 1/3 cup spring garlic, finely chopped
- Fresh chopped chives, for garnish
- 3 eggs, beaten
- 1/2 teaspoon dried dill weed
- 1 teaspoon dried rosemary
- 1/3 cup scallions, chopped

- 1/3 cup smoked white fish, chopped
- 1 ½ tablespoon crème Fraiche
- 1 teaspoon kosher salt
- 1 teaspoon dried marjoram
- 1/3 teaspoon ground black pepper, or more to taste
- Cooking spray

Directions

1. Firstly, spritz four oven-safe ramekins with cooking spray. Then, divide smoked whitefish, spring garlic, and scallions among greased ramekins.
2. Crack an egg into each ramekin; add the crème, yogurt, and all seasonings.

3. Now, air-fry approximately 13 minutes at 355 degrees f. Taste for doneness and eat warm garnished with fresh chives.

Nutrition

249 Calories | 22.1g Fat | 7.6g Carbohydrates | 5.3g Protein | 3.1g Sugars | 0.7g Fiber

147. Parmesan and Paprika Baked Tilapia

⏰ Prep Time 20 m | ⏱ Cooking Time 15 m | 6 Servings

Ingredients

- 1 cup parmesan cheese, grated
- 1 teaspoon paprika
- 1 teaspoon dried dill weed
- 2 pounds tilapia fillets
- 1/3 cup mayonnaise
- 1/2 tablespoon lime juice
- Salt and ground black pepper, to taste

Directions

1. Mix the mayonnaise, parmesan, paprika, salt, black pepper, and dill weed until everything is thoroughly combined.
2. Then, drizzle tilapia fillets with the lime juice.
3. Cover each fish fillet with parmesan mayo mixture; roll them in parmesan paprika mixture. Bake to your fryer at 335 for about 10 minutes. Serve and eat warm.

Nutrition

294 calories | 16.1g fat | 2.7g Carbohydrates | 35.9g protein | 0.1g sugars | 0.2g fiber

148. Tangy Cod Fillets

⏰ Prep Time 20 m | ⏱ Cooking Time 15 m | 2 Servings

Ingredients

1 ½ tablespoons sesame oil

1/2 heaping teaspoon dried parsley flakes

1/3 teaspoon fresh lemon zest, finely grated

2 medium-sized cod fillets

1 teaspoon sea salt flakes

A pinch of salt and pepper

1/3 teaspoon ground black pepper, or more to savor

1/2 tablespoon fresh lemon juice

Directions

1. Set the air fryer to cook at 375 degrees f. Season each cod fillet with sea salt flakes, black pepper, and dried parsley flakes. Now, drizzle them with sesame oil.
2. Place the seasoned cod fillets in a single layer at the bottom of the cooking basket; air-fry approximately 10 minutes.
3. While the fillets are cooking, prepare the sauce by mixing the other ingredients. Serve cod fillets on four individual plates garnished with the creamy citrus sauce.

Nutrition

291 calories | 11.1g fat | 2.7g Carbohydrates | 41.6g protein | 1.2g sugars | 0.5g fiber

149. Fish and Cauliflower Cakes

⏰ Prep Time 2 h 20 m | ⏱ Cooking Time 13 m | 4 Servings

Ingredients

- 1/2-pound cauliflower florets
- 1/2 teaspoon English mustard
- 2 tablespoons butter, room temperature
- 1/2 tablespoon cilantro, minced

- 2 tablespoons sour cream
- 2 ½ cups cooked white fish
- Salt and freshly cracked black pepper, to savor

Directions

1. Boil the cauliflower until tender. Then, purée the cauliflower in your blender. Transfer to a mixing dish.

2. Now, stir in the fish, cilantro, salt, and black pepper.

3. Add the sour cream, English mustard, and butter; mix until everything's well incorporated. Using your hands, shape into patties.

4. Place inside the refrigerator for around two hours. Cook in your fryer for 13 minutes at 395 degrees F. Serve with some extra English mustard.

Nutrition

285 calories | 15.1g fat | 4.3g Carbohydrates | 31.1g protein | 1.6g sugars | 1.3g fiber

Poultry Recipes

150. Honey and Wine Chicken Breasts

⏱ Prep Time 5 m | ⏱ Cooking Time 15 m | 4 Servings

Ingredients

- 2 chicken breasts, rinsed and halved
- 1 tablespoon melted butter
- A pinch of salt and 1/2 tsp freshly ground pepper to taste
- 3/4 teaspoon sea salt, or to taste

- 1 teaspoon paprika
- 1 teaspoon dried rosemary
- 2 tablespoons dry white wine
- 1 tablespoon honey

Directions

1. Firstly, pat the chicken breasts dry. Lightly coat them with the melted butter.
2. Then, add the remaining ingredients.

3. Transfer them to the air fryer rack/basket; bake about 15 minutes at 330 degrees F. Serve warm and enjoy

Nutrition

Calories 189 | Fat: 14g | Protein:11g | Sugar:1 g

151. Crispy Honey Garlic Chicken Wings

⏱ Prep Time 10 m | ⏱ Cooking Time 25 m | 8 Servings

Ingredients

- 1/8 C. water
- ½ tsp. salt
- 4 tbsp. minced garlic
- ¼ C. vegan butter

- ¼ C. raw honey
- ¾ C. almond flour
- 16 chicken wings

Directions

1. Rinse off and dry chicken wings well.
2. Spray air fryer rack/basket with olive oil.
3. Coat chicken wings with almond flour and add coated wings to the Air fryer oven.
4. Set temperature to 380°F, and set time to 25 minutes. Cook shaking every 5 minutes.
5. When the timer goes off, cook 5-10 minutes at 400 degrees till the skin becomes crispy and dry.

6. As chicken cooks, melt butter in a saucepan and add garlic. Sauté garlic 5 minutes. Add salt and honey, simmer 20 minutes. Make sure to stir every so often, so the sauce does not burn. Add a bit of water after 15 minutes to ensure the sauce does not harden.
7. Take out chicken wings from the air fryer and coat in sauce. Enjoy!

Nutrition

Calories: 435 | Fat: 19g | Protein:31g | Sugar 6 g

152. Lemon-Pepper Chicken Wings

⏰ Prep Time 10 m | ⏰ Cooking Time 20 m | 4 Servings

Ingredients

- 8 whole chicken wings
- Juice of ½ lemon
- ½ teaspoon garlic powder
- 1 teaspoon onion powder
- Salt
- Pepper
- ¼ cup low-fat buttermilk
- ½ cup all-purpose flour
- Cooking oil

Directions

1. Place the wings in a sealed plastic bag. Drizzle the wings with the lemon juice. Season the wings with the garlic powder, onion powder, and salt and pepper to taste.
2. Seal the bag. Shake thoroughly to combine the seasonings and coat the wings.
3. Pour the buttermilk and the flour into separate bowls large enough to dip the wings.
4. Spray the oven rack/basket with cooking oil.
5. One at a time, dip the wings in the buttermilk and then the flour.
6. Place the wings in the oven rack/basket. It is okay to stack them on top of each other. Spray the wings with cooking oil, being sure to spray the bottom layer. Place the tray rack on the middle shelf of the Air fryer oven. Set temperature to 360°F and cook for 5 minutes.
7. Remove the basket and shake it to ensure all of the pieces will cook fully.
8. Return the basket to the Air fryer oven and continue to cook the chicken. Repeat shaking every 5 minutes until a total of 20 minutes has passed.
9. Cool before serving.

Nutrition

Calories: 347 | Fat: 12g | Protein:46g | Fiber:1g

153. Cheesy Chicken in Leek-Tomato Sauce

⏰ Prep Time 10 m | ⏰ Cooking Time 20 m | 4 Servings

Ingredients

- Large-sized chicken breasts, cut in half lengthwise
- Salt and ground black pepper, to taste
- Ounces cheddar cheese, cut into sticks
- 1 tablespoon sesame oil
- 1 cup leeks, chopped
- 2 cloves garlic, minced
- 2/3 cup roasted vegetable stock
- 2/3 cup tomato puree
- 1 teaspoon dried rosemary
- 1 teaspoon dried thyme

Directions

1. Firstly, season chicken breasts with the salt and black pepper; place a piece of cheddar cheese in the middle. Then, tie it using a kitchen string; drizzle with sesame oil and reserve.
2. Add the leeks and garlic to the oven-safe bowl.
3. Cook in the Air fryer oven at 390 degrees F for 5 minutes or until tender.
4. Add the reserved chicken. Throw in the other ingredients and cook for 12 to 13 minutes more or until the chicken is done. Enjoy!

154. Mexican Chicken Burgers

⏲ Prep Time 10 m | ⏲ Cooking Time 10 m | 6 Servings

Ingredients

- 1 jalapeno pepper
- 1 tsp. cayenne pepper
- 1 tbsp. mustard powder
- 1 tbsp. oregano
- 1 tbsp. thyme

- 3 tbsp. smoked paprika
- 1 beaten egg
- 1 small head of cauliflower
- Chicken breasts

Directions

1. Ensure your Air fryer oven is preheated to 350 degrees.
2. Add seasonings to a blender. Slice cauliflower into florets and add to blender.
3. Pulse till mixture resembles that of breadcrumbs.
4. Take out ¾ of the cauliflower mixture and add to a bowl. Set to the side. In another bowl, beat your egg and set it to the side.
5. Remove skin and bones from chicken breasts and add to blender with remaining cauliflower mixture. Season with pepper and salt.
6. Take out the mixture and form into burger shapes. Roll each patty in cauliflower crumbs, then the egg, and back into crumbs again.
7. Place coated patties into the Air fryer oven. Set temperature to 350°F, and set time to 10 minutes.
8. Flip over at a 10-minute mark. They are done when crispy!

Nutrition

Calories: 234 | Fat: 18g | Protein: 24g | Sugar: 1g

155. Fried Chicken Livers

⏲ Prep Time 5 m | ⏲ Cooking Time 10 m | 4 Servings

Ingredients

- 1 pound chicken livers
- 1 cup flour
- 1/2 cup cornmeal

- 2 teaspoons your favorite seasoning blend
- eggs
- 2 tablespoons milk

Directions

1. Clean and rinse the livers, pat dry.
2. Beat eggs in a shallow bowl and mix in milk.
3. In another bowl combine flour, cornmeal, and seasoning, mixing until even.
4. Dip the livers in the egg mix, then toss them in the flour mix.
5. Air-fry at 375 degrees for 10 minutes using your Air fryer oven. Toss at least once halfway through.

Nutrition

Calories 409 | Fat 11g | Protein 36g | Fiber 2g

156. Minty Chicken-Fried Pork Chops

⏰ Prep Time 10 m | ⏲ Cooking Time 30 m | 6 Servings

Ingredients

- Medium-sized pork chops, approximately 3.5 ounces each
- 1 cup of breadcrumbs (Panko brand works well)
- 2 medium-sized eggs
- Pinch of salt and pepper
- ½ tablespoon of mint, either dried and ground; or fresh, rinsed and finely chopped

Directions

1. Cover the basket of the Air fryer oven with a lining of tin foil, leaving the edges uncovered to allow air to circulate through the basket. Preheat the Air fryer oven to 350 degrees.
2. In a bowl, beat the eggs until fluffy and until the yolks and whites are completely combined and set aside.
3. In a separate bowl, combine the crumbs, mint, salt, and pepper and set aside. One at a time, dip each raw pork chop into the dry ingredient bowl, coat all sides, then dip it into the wet ingredient bowl, then dip it back into the dry ingredients. This double layer will ensure cooler air. Place the breaded pork chops on the oven rack, in a single flat layer. Place the air fryer rack on the middle shelf of the fryer.
4. Set the Air Fryer timer to 15 minutes. After 15 minutes the Air Fryer oven will turn off and the pork should cook in the middle and the bread layer should start to brown. Using tweezers, flip each piece of meat over to secure a full pair of pants. Return the fryer to 320 degrees for 15 minutes.
5. After 15 minutes, when the fryer is off, remove the fried pork chops with tongs and place them in a source. Eat as fresh as you can, and enjoy it!

Nutrition

Calories 213 | Fat 9g | Protein 12g | Fiber 3g

157. Crispy Southern Fried Chicken

⏰ Prep Time 10 m | ⏲ Cooking Time 25 m | 4 Servings

Ingredients

- 1 tsp. cayenne pepper
- 2 tbsp. mustard powder
- 2 tbsp. oregano
- 2 tbsp. thyme
- 3 tbsp. coconut milk
- 1 beaten egg
- ¼ C. cauliflower
- ¼ C. gluten-free oats
- 8 chicken drumsticks

Directions

1. Ensure the Air fryer oven is preheated to 350 degrees.
2. Lay out the chicken and season with pepper and salt on all sides.
3. Add all other ingredients to a blender, blending till a smooth-like breadcrumb mixture is created. Place in a bowl and add a beaten egg to another bowl.
4. Dip chicken into breadcrumbs, then into the egg, and breadcrumbs once more.
5. Place coated drumsticks into the Air fryer oven. Set temperature to 350°F, and set time to 20 minutes, and cook 20 minutes. Bump up the temperature to 390 degrees and cook another 5 minutes till crispy.

Nutrition

Calories 504 | Fat 18g | Protein 35g | Sugar 5g

158. Tex-Mex Turkey Burgers

⏲ Prep Time 10 m | ⏲ Cooking Time 15 m | 4 Servings

Ingredients

- ⅓ cup finely crushed corn tortilla chips
- 1 egg, beaten
- ¼ cup salsa
- ⅓ cup shredded pepper Jack cheese
- Pinch salt
- Freshly ground black pepper
- 1 pound ground turkey
- 1 tablespoon olive oil
- 1 teaspoon paprika

Directions

1. In a small bowl, combine the tortilla chips, egg, salsa, cheese, salt, and pepper, and mix well.
2. Add the turkey and mix gently but thoroughly with clean hands.
3. Form the meat mixture into patties about ½ inch thick. Make an indentation in the center of each patty with your thumb, so the burgers don't puff up while cooking.
4. Brush the patties on each side with the olive oil and sprinkle with paprika.
5. Put in the oven rack/basket. Place the tray rack on the middle shelf of the Air fryer oven. Grill for 14 to 16 minutes or until the meat registers at least 165°F.

Nutrition

Calories 354 | Fat 21g | Protein 36g | Fiber 2g

159. Air Fryer Turkey Breast

⏲ Prep Time 5 m | ⏲ Cooking Time 60 m | 6 Servings

Ingredients

- Pepper and salt
- 1 oven-ready turkey breast
- Turkey seasonings of choice

Directions

1. Preheat the Air fryer oven to 350 degrees.
2. Season turkey with pepper, salt, and other desired seasonings.
3. Place turkey in the oven rack/basket. Place the tray Rack on the middle-shelf of the Air fryer oven.
4. Set temperature to 350°F, and set time to 60 minutes. Cook 60 minutes. The meat should be at 165 degrees when done.
5. Allow resting 10-15 minutes before slicing. Enjoy!

Nutrition

Calories 212 | Fat 12g | Protein 24g | Sugar 0g

160. Mustard Chicken Tenders

⏰ Prep Time 5 m | ⏰ Cooking Time 20 m | 4 Servings

Ingredients

- ½ C. coconut flour
- 1 tbsp. spicy brown mustard
- Beaten eggs
- 1 pound of chicken tenders

Directions

1. Season tenders with pepper and salt.
2. Place a thin layer of mustard onto tenders and then dredge in flour and dip in egg.
3. Add to the Air fryer oven, set the temperature to 390°F, and set time to 20 minutes.

Nutrition

Calories 403 | Fat 20g | Protein 22g | Sugar 4g

161. Chicken Nuggets

⏰ Prep Time 10 m | ⏰ Cooking Time 20 m | 4 Servings

Ingredients

- 1 pound boneless, skinless chicken breasts
- Chicken seasoning or rub
- Salt
- Pepper
- Eggs
- Tablespoons bread crumbs
- Tablespoons panko bread crumbs
- Cooking oil

Directions

1. Cut the chicken breasts into 1-inch pieces.
2. In a large bowl, add together the chicken pieces with the chicken seasoning, salt, and pepper.
3. In a small bowl, beat the eggs. In another bowl, combine breadcrumbs and countertop.
4. Dip the chicken pieces in the eggs and then the breadcrumbs.
5. Place the pepitas in the deep fryer. Don't overdo the basket. Cook in batches. Drizzle the seeds with cooking oil.
6. Cook for 4 minutes. Open the air fryer oven and shake the basket. Set temperature to 360°F. Cook for an additional 4 minutes. Remove the cooked nuggets from the air fryer oven, then repeat steps 5 and 6 for the remaining chicken nuggets. Cool before serving.

Nutrition

Calories 206 | Fat 5g | Protein 31g | Fiber 1g

162. Cheesy Chicken Fritters

⏰ Prep Time 5 m | ⏱ Cooking Time 20 m | 17 Servings

Ingredients

Chicken Fritters:

- ½ tsp. salt
- 1/8 tsp. pepper
- 1 ½ tbsp. fresh dill
- 1 1/3 C. shredded mozzarella cheese
- 1/3 C. coconut flour
- 1/3 C. vegan mayo
- 2 eggs
- 1 ½ pounds chicken breasts

Garlic Dip:

- 1/8 tsp. pepper
- ¼ tsp. salt
- ½ tbsp. lemon juice
- 1 pressed garlic cloves
- 1/3 C. vegan mayo

Directions

1. Slice chicken breasts into 1/3" pieces and place in a bowl. Add all remaining fritter ingredients to the bowl and stir well. Cover and chill 2 hours or overnight.
2. Ensure your air fryer is preheated to 350 degrees. Spray basket with a bit of olive oil.
3. Add marinated chicken to the air fryer oven. Set temperature to 350°F, and set time to 20 minutes and cook 20 minutes, making sure to turn halfway through the cooking process.
4. To make the dipping sauce, combine all the dip ingredients until smooth.

Nutrition

Calories 467 | Fat 27g | Protein 21g | Sugar 3g

163. Air Fryer Chicken Parmesan

⏰ Prep Time 5 m | ⏱ Cooking Time 9 m | 4 Servings

Ingredients

- ½ C. keto marinara
- tbsp. mozzarella cheese
- 1 tbsp. melted ghee
- tbsp. grated parmesan cheese
- tbsp. gluten-free seasoned breadcrumbs
- 8-ounce chicken breasts

Directions

1. Ensure air fryer is preheated to 360 degrees. Spray the basket with olive oil.
2. Mix parmesan cheese and breadcrumbs together. Melt ghee.
3. Brush melted ghee onto the chicken and dip into breadcrumb mixture.
4. Place coated chicken in the air fryer and top with olive oil.
5. Set temperature to 360°F, and set time to 6 minutes. Cook 2 breasts for 6 minutes and top each breast with a tablespoon of sauce and 1½ tablespoons of mozzarella cheese. Cook another 3 minutes to melt the cheese.
6. Keep cooked pieces warm as you repeat the process with remaining breasts.

Nutrition

Calories 251 | Fat 10g | Protein 31g | Sugar 0g

164. Ricotta and Parsley Stuffed Turkey Breasts

⏰ Prep Time 5 m | ⏱ Cooking Time 25 m | 4 Servings

Ingredients

- 1 turkey breast, quartered
- 1 cup Ricotta cheese
- 1/4 cup fresh Italian parsley, chopped
- 1 teaspoon garlic powder
- 1/2 teaspoon cumin powder

- 1 egg, beaten
- 1 teaspoon paprika
- Salt and ground black pepper, to taste
- Crushed tortilla chips
- 1 ½ tablespoons extra-virgin olive oil

Directions

1. Firstly, flatten out each piece of turkey breast with a rolling pin. Prepare three mixing bowls.

2. In a shallow bowl, combine Ricotta cheese with the parsley, garlic powder, and cumin powder.

3. Place the Ricotta/parsley mixture in the middle of each piece. Repeat with the remaining pieces of the turkey breast and roll them up.

4. In another shallow bowl, whisk the egg together with paprika. In the third shallow bowl, combine the salt, pepper, and crushed tortilla chips.

5. Dip each roll in the whisked egg, then, roll them over the tortilla chips mixture.

6. Transfer prepared rolls to the oven rack/basket. Drizzle olive oil over all the rolls. Place the tray Rack on the middle-shelf of the Air fryer oven.

7. Cook for 25 minutes at 350 degrees F, working in batches. Serve warm, garnished with some extra parsley, if desired.

Nutrition

Calories 509 | Fat 23g | Protein 26g | Fiber 5g

Appetizers

165. Steamed Pot Stickers

⏲ Prep Time 20 m | ⏲ Cooking Time 10 m | 30 Servings

Ingredients

- ½ cup finely chopped cabbage
- 2 teaspoons low-sodium soy sauce
- 2 tablespoons cocktail sauce
- 30 wonton wrappers

- ¼ cup finely chopped red bell pepper
- 3 tablespoons water, and more for brushing the wrappers
- 2 green onions, finely chopped
- 1 egg, beaten

Directions

1. Combine the cabbage, bell pepper, chives, egg, cocktail sauce in a small bowl, and soy sauce and mix well.
2. Put exactly 1 teaspoon of the mixture in the middle of each wonton wrapper. Fold the wrap in half, covering the filling. wet the edges with water and seal. You can fold the edges of the wrapper with your fingers so they look like the stickers you get at restaurants. Brush them with water.

3. Put 3 tablespoons of water in the skillet under the fryer basket. Cook potstickers in 2 batches for 9 to 10 minutes or until potstickers are hot and the bottom is light.
4. Substitution Tip: Use other veggies in this recipe, like chopped corn, peas, or zucchini, or squash in the summer. You can also add the rest of the cooked meat, such as minced pork or chicken.

Nutrition

Calories 291 | Fat 2g | Saturated Fat 0g | Cholesterol 35mg | Sodium 649mg | Carbohydrates 57g | Fiber 3g | Protein 10g

166. Beef and Mango Skewers

⏲ Prep Time 10 m | ⏲ Cooking Time 5 m | 4 Servings

Ingredients

- 2 tablespoons balsamic vinegar
- 1 tablespoon olive oil
- 1 tablespoon honey
- ½ teaspoon dried marjoram

- A pinch of salt
- Freshly ground black pepper
- 1 mango
- ¾ pound beef sirloin (cut into 1-inch cubes)

Directions

1. Put the meat cubes in a medium bowl and add the balsamic vinegar, olive oil, honey, marjoram, salt, and pepper. Mix well and then massage the marinade into the meat with your hands. Set aside.
2. To prepare the mango, leave it last and cut the skin with a sharp blade.

3. Then gently cut around the oval pit to remove the pulp. Cut the mango into 1-inch cubes.
4. The metal wire skewers alternate with three cubes of meat and two cubes of mango.
5. Bake the skewers in the skillet for 4 to 7 minutes or until the meat is browned and at least 145 ° F.

Nutrition

Calories 242 | Fat 9g | Saturated Fat 3g | Cholesterol 76mg | Sodium 96mg | Carbohydrates 13g | Fiber 1g | Protein 26g

167. Curried Sweet Potato Fries

☉ Prep Time 5 m | ☉ Cooking Time 12 m | 4 Servings

Ingredients

- ½ cup sour cream
- ½ cup mango chutney
- 3 teaspoons curry powder, divided
- 4 cups frozen sweet potato fries
- 1 tablespoon olive oil
- A pinch of salt
- Freshly ground black pepper

Directions

1. In a bowl, add together sour cream, chutney, and 1½ teaspoon curry powder. Mix well and let stand.
2. Place the sweet potatoes in a sizeable bowl. Pour over the olive oil and sprinkle with the remaining 1½ teaspoon curry powder, salt, and pepper.
3. Put the potatoes in the fryer basket. Cook 8 to 12 minutes or until crisp, hot and golden, shaking the basket once during cooking.
4. Place the potatoes in a basket and serve with the teaspoon.
5. Substitution Tip: You can choose to use fresh sweet potatoes instead of frozen potatoes. Take one or two sweet potatoes, peel them, and cut them into 1-inch-thick strips with a sharp knife or mandolin. Use according to the recipe instructions. but you will need to increase the time for cooking.

Nutrition

Calories 323 | Fat 10g | Saturated Fat 4g | Cholesterol 13mg | Sodium 138mg | Carbohydrates 58g | Fiber 7g | Protein 3g

168. Spicy Kale Chips with Yogurt Sauce

☉ Prep Time 10 m | ☉ Cooking Time 5 m | 4 Servings

Ingredients

- 1 cup Greek yogurt
- 3 tablespoons lemon juice
- 2 tablespoons honey mustard
- ½ teaspoon dried oregano
- 1 bunch curly kale
- 2 tablespoons olive oil
- ½ teaspoon salt
- ⅛ teaspoon pepper

Directions

1. In a bowl, add together the yogurt, lemon juice, honey mustard, and oregano and set aside.
2. Remove the stems and ribs from the cabbage with a sharp knife. Cut the leaves into 2 to 3-inch pieces.
3. Toss the cabbage with olive oil, salt, and pepper. Massage the oil with your hands.
4. Fry the kale in batches until crisp, about 5 minutes, shaking the basket once during cooking. Serve with yogurt sauce.

Ingredient Tip: Kale is available in different varieties. Tuscan (also known as dinosaur or lacinato) is the most powerful and makes excellent marks. Kale, the variety widely found in grocery stores, can be slightly frozen when cooked in the deep fryer, but it's still delicious.

Nutrition

Calories 154 | Fat 8g | Saturated Fat 2g | Cholesterol 3mg | Sodium 378mg | Carbohydrates 13g | Fiber 1g | Protein 8g

169. Phyllo Artichoke Triangles

⏰ Prep Time 15 m | ⏱ Cooking Time 9 m | 18 Servings

Ingredients

- ¼ cup ricotta cheese
- 1 egg white
- ⅓ cup minced drained artichoke hearts
- 3 tablespoons grated mozzarella cheese
- ½ teaspoon dried thyme
- 6 sheets frozen phyllo dough, thawed
- 2 tablespoons melted butter

Directions

1. In a bowl, combine ricotta cheese, egg white, artichoke hearts, mozzarella cheese, and thyme and mix well.

2. Cover the dough with a damp kitchen towel while you work so it doesn't dry out. Using one sheet at a time, lay it out on your work surface and cut into thirds lengthwise.

3. Apply 1½ tsp of filling on each strip at the base. Fold the bottom-right edge of the sheet over the filling to meet the other side in a triangle, then continue folding into a triangle. Brush each angle with butter to seal the edges. Repeat with the remaining dough and filling.

4. Bake, 7 at a time, for about 3 to 4 minutes or until the sex is golden and crisp.

5. Replacement Tip: You can use anything in this filling in place of artichoke hearts. Try spinach, minced shrimp, cooked sausage or keep vegetarian and use all the grated cheese.

Nutrition

Calories 271 | Fat 17g | Saturated Fat 7g | Cholesterol 19mg | Sodium 232mg | Carbohydrates 23g | Fiber 5g | Protein 9g

170. Arancini

⏰ Prep Time 15 m | ⏱ Cooking Time 22 m | 16 Servings

Ingredients

- 2 eggs, beaten
- 1½ cups panko bread crumbs, divided
- ½ cup grated Parmesan cheese
- 2 tablespoons minced fresh basil
- 2 cups cooked rice or leftover risotto
- 16 ¾-inch cubes mozzarella cheese
- 2 tablespoons olive oil

Directions

1. In a medium bowl, add together the rice, eggs, a cup of breadcrumbs, Parmesan, and basil. Shape this mixture into 16 1-inch balls.

2. Create a hole in each of the balls with your finger and place a cube of mozzarella. Glue the rice mixture firmly around the cheese.

3. On a shallow plate, add together the remaining 1 cup of breadcrumbs with the olive oil and mix well. Wrap the rice balls in the breadcrumbs for color.

4. Cook the arancini in batches for 8 to 11 minutes or until golden brown.

Did you know that in Italy, arancini, also called frittata or rice soup, is sold on the street as a snack? They have grown much larger in this country, the size of an orange, and are often cone-shaped.

Nutrition

Calories 378 | Fat: 11g | Saturated Fat 4g | Cholesterol 57mg | Sodium 361mg | Carbohydrates 53g | Fiber 2g | Protein 16g

171. Pesto Bruschetta

☿ Prep Time 10 m | ☿ Cooking Time 8 m | 4 Servings

Ingredients

- 8 slices French bread, ½ inch thick
- 2 tablespoons softened butter
- 1 cup shredded mozzarella cheese
- ½ cup basil pesto
- 1 cup chopped grape tomatoes
- 2 green onions, thinly sliced

Directions

1. Butter the bread and place the butter in the deep fryer basket. Bake 3 to 5 minutes or until bread is lightly golden.
2. Take the bread out of the basket and fill each piece with a little cheese. Return to the basket in batches and bake until cheese is melted, for about 1 to 3 minutes.
3. Meanwhile, combine pesto, tomatoes, and chives in a small bowl.
4. When the cheese is melted, remove the bread from the fryer and place it on a plate. Fill each slice with a little pesto mix and serve.

Nutrition

Calories: 462| Fat 25g|Saturated Fat 10g|Cholesterol 38mg|Sodium 822mg |Carbohydrates 41g|Fiber 3g|Protein 19g

172. Fried Tortellini with Spicy Dipping Sauce

☿ Prep Time 8 m | ☿ Cooking Time 20 m | 4 Servings

Ingredients

- ¾ cup mayonnaise
- 2 tablespoons mustard
- 1 egg
- ½ cup flour
- ½ teaspoon dried oregano
- 1½ cups bread crumbs
- 2 tablespoons olive oil
- 2 cups frozen cheese tortellini

Directions

1. In a small bowl, add together the mayonnaise and mustard and mix well. Set aside.
2. In a shallow bowl, beat the egg. In a separate bowl, combine the flour and oregano. In another bowl, combine the breadcrumbs and olive oil and mix well.
3. Add the tortellini, a few at a time, to the egg, then the flour, then the egg again, then the breadcrumbs to coat. Place in the fryer basket, cooking in batches.
4. Air fry for about 10 minutes, stirring halfway through cooking time, or until tortellini are crisp and golden on the outside. Serve with mayonnaise.

Nutrition

Calories 698| Fat 31g|Saturated Fat 4g|Cholesterol 66mg|Sodium 832mg|Carbohydrates 88g|Fiber 3g|Protein 18g

173. Shrimp Toast

⏰ Prep Time 15 m | ⏰ Cooking Time 12 m | 12 Servings

Ingredients

- 3 slices firm white bread
- ⅔ cup finely chopped peeled and deveined raw shrimp
- 1 egg white
- 2 cloves garlic, minced
- 2 tablespoons cornstarch

- ¼ teaspoon ground ginger
- A pinch of salt
- Freshly ground black pepper
- 2 tablespoons olive oil

Directions

1. Cut the crust from the bread with a sharp knife. crumble the crusts to make breadcrumbs. Set aside.
2. In a small bowl, add together the shrimp, egg white, garlic, cornstarch, ginger, salt, and pepper and mix well.
3. Spread the shrimp mixture evenly over the pan around the edges. With a sharp blade or knife, cut each slice into 4 strips.
4. Mix the breadcrumbs with the olive oil and beat with the shrimp mixture. Arrange the shrimp tostadas in the fryer basket in one layer. You may need to cook in batches.
5. Air fry for 3 to 6 minutes, until crisp and golden.

Substitution Tip: Replace the minced crab with minced shrimp in this recipe or use ground chicken or turkey.

Nutrition

Calories 121 | Fat 6g | Saturated Fat 1g | Cholesterol 72mg | Sodium 158mg | Carbohydrates 7g | Fiber 0g | Protein 9g

174. Bacon Tater Tots

⏰ Prep Time 5 m | ⏰ Cooking Time 17 m | 4 Servings

Ingredients

- 24 frozen tater tots
- 6 slices precooked bacon

- 2 tablespoons maple syrup
- 1 cup shredded Cheddar cheese

Directions

1. Put the tattoos in the fryer basket. Fry for 10 minutes, shaking the fryer basket halfway through the cooking time.
2. Cut the bacon into 1-inch pieces and slice the cheese.
3. Remove the hook from the fryer basket and place it in a 6-by-6-by-2-inch pot. Fill the bacon with the maple syrup. Air fry 5 minutes or until spoons and bacon are crisp.
4. Fill with cheese and air fry for 2 minutes or until cheese is melted.
5. Ingredient Tip: Use only precooked bacon that does not need refrigeration for this recipe. If you use regular bacon, it will emit too much fat and the cookies will end up runny, not crisp.

Nutrition

Calories: 374 | Fat: 22g | Saturated Fat: 9g | Cholesterol: 40mg | Sodium: 857mg | Carbohydrates: 34g | Fiber: 2g | Protein: 13g

175. Hash Brown Bruschetta

⏱ Prep Time 7 m | ⏱ Cooking Time 8 m | 4 Servings

Ingredients

- 4 frozen hash brown patties
- 1 tablespoon olive oil
- ⅓ cup chopped cherry tomatoes
- 3 tablespoons diced fresh mozzarella

- 2 tablespoons grated Parmesan cheese
- 1 tablespoon balsamic vinegar
- 1 tablespoon minced fresh basil

Directions

1. Place the brown cake patties in the air fryer in a single layer. Air fry for 8 minutes or until the potatoes are crisp, hot, and golden.
2. Meanwhile, combine olive oil, tomatoes, mozzarella, Parmesan, vinegar, and basil in a small bowl.

3. When the potatoes are cooked, carefully remove them from the basket and place them on a plate. Fill with tomato mixture and serve.

Nutrition

Calories: 123 | Total Fat: 6g | Saturated Fat: 2g | Cholesterol: 6mg | Sodium: 81mg | Carbohydrates: 14g | Fiber: 2g | Protein: 5g

176. Waffle Fry Poutine

⏱ Prep Time 10 m | ⏱ Cooking Time 17 m | 4 Servings

Ingredients

- 2 cups frozen waffle cut fries
- 2 teaspoons olive oil
- 1 red bell pepper, chopped

- 2 green onions, sliced
- 1 cup shredded Swiss cheese
- ½ cup bottled chicken gravy

Directions

1. Toss the waffle fries with olive oil and place it in the air fryer basket. Air-fry for 10 to 12 minutes or until the fries are crisp and light golden brown, shaking the basket halfway through the cooking time.
2. Transfer the potatoes to a 6-by-6 by 2-inch skillet and top with the bell pepper, green onions, and cheese. Air fry for 3 minutes until vegetables are crisp and soft.

3. Remove the skillet from the fryer and sprinkle the broth over the potatoes. Air fry for 2 minutes or until the broth is lukewarm. Serve immediately.

Substitution Tip: You can also make this recipe with regular frozen fries, but they may take a few more minutes to cook. Use your favorite cheese in this rich recipe.

Nutrition

Calories: 347 | Total Fat: 19g | Saturated Fat: 7g | Cholesterol: 26mg | Sodium: 435mg | Carbohydrates: 33g | Fiber: 4g | Protein: 12g

177. Crispy Beef Cubes

⏰ Prep Time 10 m | ⏱ Cooking Time 16 m | 4 Servings

Ingredients

- 1 cup cheese pasta sauce (from a 16-ounce jar)
- 1½ cups soft bread crumbs
- 2 tablespoons olive oil
- ½ teaspoon dried marjoram
- 1 pound sirloin, cut into 1-inch cubes

Directions

1. In a medium bowl, mix the meat with the pasta sauce to coat.
2. In a shallow bowl, combine the pieces of bread, oil, and marjoram and mix well. Add the meat cubes, one at a time, to the bread mixture to coat well.
3. Cook meat in two batches for 6 to 8 minutes, shaking basket once during cooking, until meat is at least 145 ° F and outside is crisp and golden. Serve with toothpicks or small forks.
4. Cooking Tip: You can use the rest of the pasta sauce to make a quick meal. Just cook one cup or two of pasta while reheating the sauce in a saucepan. Combine and enjoy.

Nutrition

Calories: 554 | Fat: 22g | Saturated Fat: 8g | Cholesterol: 112mg | Sodium: 1,832mg | Carbohydrates: 43g | Fiber: 2g | Protein: 44g

178. Buffalo Chicken Bites

⏰ Prep Time 10 m | ⏱ Cooking Time 18 m | 4 Servings

Ingredients

- ⅔ cup sour cream
- ¼ cup creamy blue cheese salad dressing
- ¼ cup crumbled blue cheese
- 3 tablespoons Buffalo chicken wing sauce
- 1 cup panko bread crumbs
- 2 tbsp. olive oil
- 1 celery stalk, finely chopped
- A pound of chicken tenders, cut into three

Directions

1. In a small bowl, add together salad dressing, sour cream, blue cheese, and celery and set aside.
2. In a medium bowl, combine chicken pieces and chicken wing sauce and toss to coat. Let stand while you prepare the ready breadcrumbs.
3. Combine the breadcrumbs and olive oil on a plate and mix.
4. Top the chicken pieces with the bread mixture, beating each piece so the crumbs stick together.
5. Fry in batches for 7 to 9 minutes, shaking basket once until chicken is cooked to 165 ° F and golden brown. Serve with the blue cheese sauce on the side.
6. Did you know that Buffalo chicken wings were first invented at Anchor Bar in Buffalo, New York, when the owner had to serve many appetizers in a hurry? It became an immediate hit and the flavor, a combination of hot sauce with fresh blue cheese, is now a classic.

Nutrition

Calories: 467 | Fat: 23g | Saturated Fat: 8g | Cholesterol: 119mg | Sodium: 821mg | Carbohydrates: 22g | Fiber: 1g | Protein: 43g

179. Sweet and Hot Chicken Wings

⏰ Prep Time 5 m | ⏰ Cooking Time 25 m | 16 Servings

Ingredients

- 8 chicken wings
- 1 tablespoon olive oil
- ⅓ cup brown sugar
- 2 tablespoons honey
- ⅓ cup apple cider vinegar
- 2 cloves garlic, minced
- ½ teaspoon dried red pepper flakes
- ¼ teaspoon salt

Directions

1. Cut each chicken wing into three pieces. You will have a large piece, a middle piece, and a small tip. Discard the small tip or save it for stock.
2. In a medium bowl, rub the wings with the oil. Transfer to the fryer basket and cook for 20 minutes, shaking the basket twice while cooking.
3. Also, in a small bowl, combine the honey, vinegar, red pepper flakes, sugar, and salt and mix until just combined.
4. Remove the feathers from the fryer basket and place them in a 6-by-6-inch pot. Pour the sauce over the wings and pour.
5. Return to the fryer and cook for 5 minutes or until the wings are polished.
6. Ingredient Tip: You can sometimes buy "chicken drums" in the meat section. They are made from chicken meat. If you want to use these instead of cutting whole feathers, use about 10 in this recipe.

Nutrition

Calories 438 | Fat 16g | Saturated Fat 4g | Cholesterol 151mg | Sodium 299mg | Carbohydrates 21g | Fiber 0g | Protein 49g

Paleo Recipes

180. Healthy Brussels Sprouts

⏱ Prep Time 8 m | ⏱ Cooking Time 12 m | 3 Servings

Ingredients

- 8 oz. Brussels sprouts
- 1/2 tsp garlic powder
- 1/2 tsp salt
- 1/4 tsp black pepper
- 1 tsp olive oil

Directions

1. Rinse Brussels sprout into the water and dry with a paper towel.
2. Cut Brussels sprouts bottom stem and cut them in half and place them into the bowl.
3. Toss sprouts with garlic powder, salt, pepper, and olive oil and put them into the air fryer basket.
4. Air fry them until they are slightly brown at 360 F/ 182 C for 12 minutes. Shake the air fryer basket halfway through.
5. Transfer Brussels sprouts to the plate and drizzle with fresh lime juice.
6. Serve and enjoy.

Nutrition

Calories 167 | Carbohydrates 7.8g | Protein 32.1g | Fat 15g

181. Mediterranean Vegetables

⏱ Prep Time 5 m | ⏱ Cooking Time 15 m | 2 Servings

Ingredients

- 1/3 cup cherry tomatoes
- 1 parsnip, peel and diced
- 1 carrot, peel and diced
- 1 courgette, sliced
- 1 green pepper, sliced
- 1 tsp mustard
- 1 tsp mixed herbs
- 2 tbsp. honey
- 6 tbsp. olive oil
- 2 tsp garlic paste
- Pepper
- Salt

Directions

1. Add all vegetables into the air fryer basket. Drizzle with 3 tbsp. oil and toss well.
2. Cook into air fryer for 15 minutes at 356 F/ 180 C.
3. Meanwhile, mix remaining ingredients into the air fryer baking dish.
4. Once vegetables are cooked then transfer them into the baking dish and toss well all.
5. Return vegetables into the air fryer basket and cook for 5 minutes more.
6. Serve and enjoy.

Nutrition

Calories 125 | Carbohydrates 8g | Protein 23.1g | Fat 7g

182. Healthy Green Beans

⏱ Prep Time 5 m | ⏱ Cooking Time 10 m | 6 Servings

Ingredients

- 2 cups green beans, cut in half
- 2 tbsp. olive oil
- 1 tbsp. shawarma spice
- 1/2 tsp salt

Directions

1. Add beans, olive oil, salt, and shawarma into the bowl and toss well.

2. Place beans into the air fryer basket for 10 minutes at 370 F/ 187 C. Shake air fryer basket halfway through.

3. Serve and enjoy.

Nutrition

Calories 243 | Carbohydrates 14g | Protein 12g | Fat 6g

183. Simple Tomatillo Salsa

⏱ Prep Time 5 m | ⏱ Cooking Time 15 m | 5 Servings

Ingredients

- 12 tomatillos wash and remove the husk
- 2 Serrano peppers, cut the stems
- 1 tbsp. olive oil
- 1 cup cilantro, chopped
- 1 tbsp. garlic, minced
- 1 tsp salt

Directions

1. Place the peppers and tomatillos into a heatproof dish and place them into the air fryer basket.

2. Cook in the oven for 15 minutes at 350 F/ 176 C.

3. Once cooking time is over then transfer tomatillos mixture into a blender and blend until pureed.

4. Pour blended mixture into the bowl. Add olive oil, garlic, and salt and stir well.

5. Serve and enjoy.

Nutrition

Calories 365 | Carbohydrates 11.8g | Protein 43.1g | Fat 10g

184. Roasted Zucchini

⏱ Prep Time 13 m | ⏱ Cooking Time 30 m | 3 Servings

Ingredients

- 16 oz. Zucchini, sliced into 1/4inch rounds
- 1 tsp garlic powder
- 1/2 tsp black pepper
- 2 tbsp. olive oil
- 1 tsp kosher salt

Directions

1. Preheat the air fryer at 400 F/ 204 C for 3 minutes.

2. Toss zucchini with olive oil, garlic powder, pepper, and salt.

3. Place seasoned zucchini into the air fryer basket and cook for 30 minutes. Shake sir fryer basket 2-3 times during cooking.

4. Serve and enjoy.

Nutrition

Calories 251 | Carbohydrates 12g | Protein 16g | Fat 2g

185. Tasty Broccoli Bites

⏱ Prep Time 10 m | ⏱ Cooking Time 5 m | 2 Servings

Ingredients

- 3 cups broccoli florets
- 1 tsp onion powder
- 1 tsp garlic powder
- 1 tsp paprika
- 2 tbsp. Nutritional yeast
- 2 tbsp. olive oil
- Pepper
- Salt

Directions

1. Preheat air fryer at 392 F/ 200 C.
2. Add all ingredients into the mixing bowl and toss well to coat.
3. Add broccoli in the air fryer basket and cook for 4-5 minutes.
4. Serve and enjoy.

Nutrition

Calories 265 | Carbohydrates 19g | Protein 22g | Fat 1g

186. Healthy Apple Chips

⏱ Prep Time 2 m | ⏱ Cooking Time 8 m | 4 Servings

Ingredients

- 1 large apple, slice using the slicer
- 1/4 tsp ground nutmeg
- 1/4 tsp ground cinnamon

Directions:

1. Preheat air fryer at 375 F/ 190 C for 3 minutes.
2. Season apple slices with nutmeg and cinnamon.
3. Place apple slice in the air fryer basket and cook for 7-8 minutes.
4. Serve and enjoy.

Nutrition

Calories 312 | Carbohydrates 20g | Protein 40g | Fat 10g

187. Zucchini Chips

⏱ Prep Time 10 m | ⏱ Cooking Time 16 m | 7 Servings

Ingredients

- 1 tbsp. olive oil
- 1 tsp Cajun seasoning
- 1 large zucchini, slice into 1/8" part

Directions

1. Place zucchini slices into the oven basket and drizzle with olive oil.
2. Sprinkle Cajun seasoning on top of zucchini slices.
3. Air-fry them for 187 C/ 370 F for 8 minutes.
4. Turn zucchini chips to the other side and cook for 8 minutes more.
5. Serve and enjoy.

Nutrition

Calories 165 | Carbohydrates 18g | Protein 31g | Fat 2g

188. Roasted Eggplant

⏱ Prep Time 10 m | ⏱ Cooking Time 20 m | 5 Servings

Ingredients

- 2 medium eggplants remove stems and cut into 1-inch pieces
- 1 tbsp. olive oil
- 1 tbsp. lemon juice
- 1 tsp garlic powder
- 1 tsp onion powder
- Pepper
- Salt

Directions

1. Add all ingredients except lemon juice into the bowl and toss well.
2. Place eggplant mixture into the air fryer basket and cook for 15 at 320 F/ 160 C.
3. Toss well and turn temperature to 350 F/ 180 C for 5 minutes.
4. Transfer cooked eggplant into the bowl and drizzle with lemon juice.
5. Serve and enjoy.

Nutrition

Calories 565 | Carbohydrates 26g | Protein 33g | Fat 6g

189. Kale Chips

⏱ Prep Time 5 m | ⏱ Cooking Time 15 m | 7 Servings

Ingredients

- 3 cups kale, wash and cut into bite-size pieces
- 1 tbsp. zaatar seasoning
- 1 tbsp. olive oil
- 1/2 tsp sea salt

Directions

1. Add all necessary ingredients into the bowl and toss well.
2. Place kale mixture into the air fryer basket and cook for 10-15 minutes at 170 C/ 338 F or until kale chips edges brown.
3. Serve and enjoy.

Nutrition

Calories 261 | Carbohydrates 16.5g | Protein 43.1g | Fat 2.3g

190. Roasted Broccoli

⏱ Prep Time 8 m | ⏱ Cooking Time 8 m | 2 Servings

Ingredients

- 3 cups broccoli florets
- 1 tbsp. olive oil
- 1 tbsp. honey
- 2 tbsp. balsamic vinegar

Directions

1. Preheat the air fryer to 374 F/ 190 C for 3 minutes.
2. Add broccoli florets into the air fryer basket and drizzle with olive oil.
3. Cook broccoli in the air fryer for 8 minutes. Shake basket halfway through.
4. Transfer cooked broccoli into the mixing bowl. Add honey and vinegar and toss well to coat.
5. Serve and enjoy.

Nutrition

Calories 276 | Carbohydrates 31g | Protein 14g | Fat 12g

191. Lemon Garlic Broccoli

⏱ Prep Time 8 m | ⏱ Cooking Time 8 m | 12 Servings

Ingredients

- 3 cups broccoli florets
- 1 tbsp. olive oil
- 2 garlic cloves, chopped
- 2 tbsp. lemon juice
- Pepper
- Salt

Directions

1. Preheat the air fryer to 374 F/190 C for 3 minutes.
2. Add broccoli florets into the air fryer basket and drizzle with olive oil.
3. Cook broccoli in the air fryer for 8 minutes. Shake basket halfway through.
4. Transfer cooked broccoli into the mixing bowl. Add garlic, lemon juice, pepper, and salt and toss well.
5. Serve and enjoy.

Nutrition

Calories 298 | Carbohydrates 11g | Protein 40g | Fat 10g

192. Roasted Carrots

⏰ Prep Time 10 m | ⏱ Cooking Time 14 m | 4 Servings

Ingredients

- 6 carrots peeled and sliced into thick chips
- 1 tbsp. oregano
- 2 tbsp. olive oil
- 1 tbsp. fresh parsley, chopped
- Pepper
- Salt

Directions

1. Add carrots into the air fryer basket and drizzle with olive oil.
2. Cook carrots in the air fryer for 12 minutes at 360 F/180 C. Shake baskets halfway through.
3. Add oregano, pepper, and salt and shake basket well and cook for 2 minutes more at 400 F/204 C.
4. Garnish with chopped parsley and serve.

Nutrition

Calories 245 | Carbohydrates 28g | Protein 11g | Fat 19g

193. Garlic Herb Rib-Eye Steak

⏰ Prep Time 8 m | ⏱ Cooking Time 12 m | 3 Servings

Ingredients

- 8 oz. ribeye steak
- 1 tsp Worcestershire sauce
- 2 tsp garlic, minced
- 2 tbsp. parsley, chopped
- 1 stick grass-fed butter, softened
- 1/2 tsp salt

Directions

1. In a bowl, mix together parsley, butter, garlic, Worcestershire sauce, and salt.
2. Rub the butter mixture all over the steak and place it in the refrigerator for 1 hour.
3. Preheat the air fryer to 400 F/204 C.
4. Place marinated steak in the air fryer basket and cook for 12 minutes.
5. Serve and enjoy.

Nutrition

Calories 203 | Carbohydrates 10g | Protein 13g | Fat 2g

194. Tasty Beef Patties

⏱ Prep Time 10 m | ⏱ Cooking Time 10 m | 5 Servings

Ingredients

- 1 lb. ground beef
- 1 tsp dried parsley
- 1/2 tsp dried oregano
- 1/2 tsp onion powder

- 1 tbsp. Worcestershire sauce
- 1/2 tsp salt
- 1/2 tsp garlic powder
- 1/2 tsp black pepper

Directions

1. Preheat the air fryer to 176 C/ 350 F.
2. In a small bowl, mix together all ingredients except meat.
3. Add ground meat into the large mixing bowl. Add seasoning mixture into the ground meat and mix until well combined.
4. Make four burger shape patties from the mixture.
5. Place patties in the air fryer basket and cook for 10 minutes.
6. Serve and enjoy.

Nutrition

Calories 250 | Carbohydrates 11g | Protein 40g | Fat 9g

Dessert Recipes

195. Angel Food Cake

⏰ Prep Time 10 m | ⏰ Cooking Time 30 m | 12 Servings

Ingredients

- ¼ cup butter, melted
- 1 cup powdered erythritol
- 1 teaspoon strawberry extract
- 12 egg whites
- 2 teaspoons cream of tartar
- A pinch of salt

Directions

1. Preheat the air fryer for 5 minutes.
2. Mix the egg whites together with the cream of tartar.
3. Use a hand mixer and whisk until white and fluffy.
4. Add the rest of the ingredients except for the butter and whisk for another minute.
5. Pour into a baking dish.
6. Place in the oven basket and cook for 30 minutes at 4000F or if a toothpick inserted in the middle comes out clean.
7. Drizzle with melted butter once cooled.

Nutrition

Calories 65 | Carbohydrates 1.8g | Protein 3.1g | Fat 5g

196. Apple Pie in Air Fryer

⏰ Prep Time 15 m | ⏰ Cooking Time 35 m | 4 Servings

Ingredients

- ½ teaspoon vanilla extract
- 1 beaten egg
- 1 large apple, chopped
- 1 Pillsbury Refrigerator pie crust
- 1 tablespoon butter
- 1 tablespoon ground cinnamon
- 1 tablespoon raw sugar
- 2 tablespoon sugar
- 2 teaspoons lemon juice
- Baking spray

Directions

1. Lightly grease baking pan of the air fryer with cooking spray. Spread the pie crust on the rare part of the pan up to the sides.
2. In a bowl, make a mixture of vanilla, sugar, cinnamon, lemon juice, and apples. Pour on top of pie crust. Top apples with butter slices.
3. Cover apples with the other pie crust. Pierce with a knife the tops of the pie.
4. Spread whisked egg on top of crust and sprinkle sugar.
5. Cover with foil.
6. For 25 minutes, cook on 390oF.
7. Remove foil cook for 10 minutes at 330oF until tops are browned.
8. Serve and enjoy.

Nutrition

Calories 372 | Carbs 44.7g | Protein 4.2g | Fat 19.6g

197. Apple-Toffee Upside-Down Cake

⏰ Prep Time 10 m | ⏱ Cooking Time 30 m | 9 Servings

Ingredients

- ¼ cup almond butter
- ¼ cup sunflower oil
- ½ cup walnuts, chopped
- ¾ cup + 3 tablespoon coconut sugar
- ¾ cup water
- 1 ½ teaspoon mixed spice
- 1 cup plain flour
- 1 lemon, zest
- 1 teaspoon baking soda
- 1 teaspoon vinegar
- 3 baking apples, cored and sliced

Directions

1. Preheat the air fryer to 3900F.
2. In a skillet, melt the almond butter and 3 tablespoons sugar. Pour the mixture over a baking dish that will fit in the air fryer. Arrange the slices of apples on top. Set aside.
3. In a mixing bowl, combine flour, ¾ cup sugar, and baking soda. Add the mixed spice.
4. In a different bowl, mix the water, oil, vinegar, and lemon zest. Stir in the chopped walnuts.
5. Combine the wet ingredients to the dry ingredients until well combined.
6. Pour over the tin with apple slices.
7. Bake for 30 minutes or until a toothpick inserted comes out clean.

Nutrition

Calories 335 | Carbohydrates 39.6g | Protein 3.8g | Fat 17.9g

198. Banana-Choco Brownies

⏰ Prep Time 15 m | ⏱ Cooking Time 30 m | 12 Servings

Ingredients

- 2 cups almond flour
- 2 teaspoons baking powder
- ½ teaspoon baking powder
- ½ teaspoon baking soda
- ½ teaspoon salt
- 1 over-ripe banana
- 3 large eggs
- ½ teaspoon stevia powder
- ¼ cup coconut oil
- 1 tablespoon vinegar
- 1/3 cup almond flour
- 1/3 cup cocoa powder

Directions

1. Preheat the air fryer for 5 minutes.
2. Add together all ingredients in a food processor and pulse until well combined.
3. Pour into a skillet that will fit in the deep fryer.
4. Place in the fryer basket and cook for 30 minutes at 3500F or if a toothpick inserted in the middle comes out clean.

Nutrition

Calories 75 | Carbohydrates 2.1g | Protein 1.7g | Fat 6.6g

199. Blueberry & Lemon Cake

⏰ Prep Time 10 m | ⏱ Cooking Time 17 m | 4 Servings

Ingredients

- 2 eggs
- 1 cup blueberries
- zest from 1 lemon
- juice from 1 lemon
- 1 tsp. vanilla

- brown sugar for topping (a little sprinkling on top of each muffin-less than a teaspoon)
- 2 1/2 cups self-rising flour
- 1/2 cup Monk Fruit (or use your preferred sugar)
- 1/2 cup cream
- 1/4 cup avocado oil (any light cooking oil)

Directions

1. In mixing bowl, beat well the wet ingredients. Stir in dry ingredients and mix thoroughly.
2. Lightly grease baking pan of the air fryer with cooking spray. Pour in batter.

3. For 12 minutes, cook on 330F.
4. Let it stand in the air fryer for 5 minutes.
5. Serve and enjoy.

Nutrition

Calories 589 | Carbs 76.7g | Protein 13.5g | Fat 25.3g

200. Bread Pudding with Cranberry

⏰ Prep Time 20 m | ⏱ Cooking Time 45 m | 4 Servings

Ingredients

- 1-1/2 cups milk
- 2-1/2 eggs
- 1/2 cup cranberries1 teaspoon butter
- 1/4 cup golden raisins
- 1/8 teaspoon ground cinnamon
- 3/4 cup heavy whipping cream

- 3/4 teaspoon lemon zest
- 3/4 teaspoon kosher salt
- 2 tbsp. and 1/4 cup white sugar
- 3/4 French baguettes, cut into 2-inch slices
- 3/8 vanilla bean, split and seeds scraped away

Directions

1. Lightly grease baking pan of the air fryer with cooking spray. Spread baguette slices, cranberries, and raisins.
2. In a blender, blend well vanilla bean, cinnamon, salt, lemon zest, eggs, sugar, and cream. Pour over baguette slices. Let it soak for an hour.

3. Cover pan with foil.
4. For 35 minutes, cook on 330F.
5. Let it rest for 10 minutes.
6. Serve and enjoy.

Nutrition

Calories 581 | Carbs 76.1g | Protein 15.8g | Fat 23.7g

201. Cherries 'n Almond Flour Bars

⏰ Prep Time 15 m | ⏱ Cooking Time 35 m | 12 Servings

Ingredients

- ¼ cup of water
- ½ cup butter softened
- ½ teaspoon salt
- ½ teaspoon vanilla
- 1 ½ cups almond flour
- 1 cup erythritol
- 1 cup fresh cherries, pitted
- 1 tablespoon xanthan gum
- 2 eggs

Directions

1. In a medium bowl, make a mixture of the first 6 ingredients to form a dough.
2. Press the batter onto a baking sheet that will fit in the air fryer.
3. Place in the fryer and bake for 10 minutes at 375F.
4. Meanwhile, mix the cherries, water, and xanthan gum in a bowl.
5. Scoop out the dough and pour over the cherry.
6. Return to the fryer and cook for another 25 minutes at 3750F.

Nutrition

Calories 99 | Carbohydrates 2.1g | Protein 1.8g | Fat 9.3g

202. Cherry-Choco Bars

⏰ Prep Time 5 m | ⏱ Cooking Time 15 m | 8 Servings

Ingredients

- ¼ teaspoon salt
- ½ cup almonds, sliced
- ½ cup chia seeds
- ½ cup dark chocolate, chopped
- ½ cup dried cherries, chopped
- ½ cup prunes, pureed
- ½ cup quinoa, cooked
- ¾ cup almond butter
- 1/3 cup honey
- 2 cups old-fashioned oats
- 2 tablespoon coconut oil

Directions

1. Preheat the air fryer to 3750F.
2. In a bowl, combine the oats, quinoa, chia seeds, almond, cherries, and chocolate.
3. In a saucepan, heat the almond butter, honey, and coconut oil.
4. Pour the butter mixture over the dry mixture. Add salt and prunes.
5. Mix until well combined.
6. Pour over a baking dish that can fit inside the air fryer.
7. Cook for 15 minutes.
8. Allow settling for an hour before slicing into bars.

Nutrition

Calories 321 | Carbohydrates 35g | Protein 7g | Fat 17g

203. Chocolate Chip in a Mug

⏱ Prep Time 10 m | ⏱ Cooking Time 20 m | 6 Servings

Ingredients

- ¼ cup walnuts, shelled and chopped
- ½ cup butter, unsalted
- ½ cup dark chocolate chips
- ½ cup erythritol
- ½ teaspoon baking soda

- ½ teaspoon salt
- 1 tablespoon vanilla extract
- 2 ½ cups almond flour
- 2 large eggs, beaten

Directions

1. Preheat the air fryer for 5 minutes.
2. Combine all ingredients in a mixing bowl.

3. Place in greased mugs.
4. Bake in the air fryer oven for 20 minutes at 3750F.

Nutrition

Calories 234 | Carbohydrates 4.9g | Protein 2.3g | Fat 22.8g

204. Choco-Peanut Mug Cake

⏱ Prep Time 10 m | ⏱ Cooking Time 20 m | 6 Servings

Ingredients

- ¼ teaspoon baking powder
- ½ teaspoon vanilla extract
- 1 egg
- 1 tablespoon heavy cream

- 1 tablespoon peanut butter
- 1 teaspoon butter, softened
- 2 tablespoon erythritol
- 2 tablespoons cocoa powder, unsweetened

Directions

1. Preheat the air fryer for 5 minutes.
2. Combine all ingredients in a mixing bowl.
3. Pour into a greased mug.

4. Place in the air fryer oven basket and cook for 20 minutes at 4000F or if a toothpick inserted in the middle comes out clean.

Nutrition

Calories 293 | Carbohydrates 8.5g | Protein 12.4g | Fat 23.3g

205. Coco-Lime Bars

⏰ Prep Time 10 m | ⏰ Cooking Time 20 m | 3 Servings

Ingredients

- ¼ cup almond flour
- ¼ cup coconut oil
- ¼ cup dried coconut flakes
- ¼ teaspoon salt
- ½ cup lime juice
- ¾ cup coconut flour
- 1 ¼ cup erythritol powder
- 1 tablespoon lime zest
- 4 eggs

Directions

1. Preheat the air fryer for 5 minutes.
2. Combine all ingredients in a mixing bowl.
3. Place in the greased mug.
4. Bake in the air fryer oven for 20 minutes at 375F.

Nutrition

Calories 506 | Carbohydrates 21.9g | Protein 19.3g | Fat 37.9g

206. Coconut 'n Almond Fat Bombs

⏰ Prep Time 5 m | ⏰ Cooking Time 15 m | 12 Servings

Ingredients

- ¼ cup almond flour
- ½ cup shredded coconut
- 1 tablespoon coconut oil
- 1 tablespoon vanilla extract
- 2 tablespoons liquid stevia
- 3 egg whites

Directions

1. Preheat the air fryer for 5 minutes.
2. Combine all ingredients in a mixing bowl.
3. Form small balls using your hands.
4. Place in the air fryer oven basket and cook for 15 minutes at 4000F.

Nutrition

Calories 23 | Carbohydrates 0.7g | Protein 1.1g | Fat 1.8g

207. Coconutty Lemon Bars

⏱ Prep Time 10 m | ⏱ Cooking Time 25 m | 12 Servings

Ingredients

- ¼ cup cashew
- ¼ cup fresh lemon juice, freshly squeezed
- ¾ cup coconut milk
- ¾ cup erythritol
- 1 cup desiccated coconut
- 1 teaspoon baking powder
- 2 eggs, beaten
- 2 tablespoons coconut oil
- A dash of salt

Directions

1. Preheat the air fryer for 5 minutes.
2. In a mixing bowl, combine all ingredients.
3. Use a hand mixer to mix everything.
4. Pour into a baking bowl that will fit in the air fryer.
5. Bake for 25 minutes at 350F or until a toothpick inserted in the middle comes out clean.

Nutrition

Calories 118 | Carbohydrates 3.9g | Protein 2.6g | Fat 10.2g

208. Coffee 'n Blueberry Cake

⏱ Prep Time 15 m | ⏱ Cooking Time 35 m | 6 Servings

Ingredients

- 1 cup white sugar
- 1 egg
- 1/2 cup butter, softened
- 1/2 cup fresh or frozen blueberries
- 1/2 cup sour cream
- 1/2 teaspoon baking powder
- 1/2 teaspoon ground cinnamon
- 1/2 teaspoon vanilla extract
- 1/4 cup brown sugar
- 1/4 cup chopped pecans
- 1/8 teaspoon salt
- 1-1/2 teaspoons confectioners' sugar for dusting
- 3/4 cup and 1 tablespoon all-purpose flour

Directions

1. In a small bowl, whisk well pecans, cinnamon, and brown sugar.
2. In a blender, blend well all wet ingredients. Add dry ingredients except for confectioner's sugar and blueberries. Blend well until smooth and creamy.
3. Lightly grease baking pan of the air fryer with cooking spray.
4. Pour half of the batter in pan. Sprinkle a little of the pecan mixture on top. Pour the remaining batter and then top with the remaining pecan mixture.
5. Cover pan with foil.
6. For 35 minutes, cook on 330oF.
7. Serve and enjoy with a dusting of confectioner's sugar.

Nutrition

Calories 471 | Carbs 59.5g | Protein 4.1g | Fat 24.0g

209. Coffee Flavored Cookie Dough

⏰ Prep Time 10 m | ⏱ Cooking Time 20 m | 12 Servings

Ingredients

- ¼ cup butter
- ¼ teaspoon xanthan gum
- ½ teaspoon coffee espresso powder
- ½ teaspoon stevia powder
- ¾ cup almond flour

- 1 egg
- 1 teaspoon vanilla
- 1/3 cup sesame seeds
- 2 tablespoons cocoa powder
- 2 tablespoons cream cheese, softened

Directions

1. Preheat the air fryer for 5 minutes.
2. Combine all ingredients in a mixing bowl.
3. Press into a baking dish that will fit in the air fryer.

4. Place in the air fryer oven basket and cook for 20 minutes at 4000F or if a toothpick inserted in the middle comes out clean.

Nutrition

Calories 88 | Carbohydrates 1.3g | Protein 1.9g | Fat 8.3g

Conclusion

Hopefully, after going through this book and trying out a couple of recipes, you will get to understand the flexibility and utility of the air fryers. It is undoubtedly a multipurpose kitchen appliance that is highly recommended to everybody as it presents one with a palatable atmosphere to enjoy fried foods that are not only delicious but healthy, cheaper, and more convenient. The use of this kitchen appliance ensures that the making of some of your favorite snacks and meals will be carried out in a stress-free manner without hassling around, which invariably legitimizes its worth and gives you value for your money.

This book will be your all-time guide to understand the basics of the air fryer because, with all the recipes mentioned in the book, you are rest assured that it will be something that you and the rest of the people around the world will enjoy for the rest of your lives. You will be able to prepare delicious and flavorsome meals that will not only be easy to carry out but tasty and healthy as well.

However, you should never limit yourself to the recipes solely mentioned in this cookbook, go on and try new things! Explore new recipes! Experiment with different ingredients, seasonings, and different methods! Create some new recipes and keep your mind open. By so doing, you will be able to get the best out of your air fryer.

We are so glad you took the leap to this healthier cooking format with us!

The air fryer truly is not a gadget that should stay on the shelf. Instead, take it out and give it a whirl when you are whipping up one of your tried-and-true recipes, or if you are starting to get your feet wet with the air frying method.

Regardless of appliances, recipes, or dietary concerns, we hope you have fun in your kitchen. Between food preparation, cooking time, and then the cleanup, a lot of time is spent in this one room, so it should be as fun as possible.

This is just the start. There are no limits to working with the air fryer, and we will explore some more recipes as well. In addition to all the great options that we talked about before, you will find that there are tasty desserts that can those sweet teeth in no time, and some great sauces and dressing so you can always be in control over the foods you eat. There are just so many options to choose from that it won't take long before you find a whole bunch of recipes to use, and before you start to wonder why you didn't get the air fryer so much sooner. There are so many things to admire about the air fryer, and it becomes an even better tool to use when you have the right recipes in place and can use them. And there are so many fantastic recipes that work well in the air fryer and can get dinner on the table in no time. We are pleased that you pursue this Air Fryer cookbook. Happy, healthy eating!